Pedagogical Peculiarities

CRITICAL ISSUES IN THE FUTURE OF LEARNING AND TEACHING

Volume 13

Series Editors:

Britt-Marie Apelgren, *University of Gothenburg, Sweden*
Pamela Burnard, *University of Cambridge, UK*
Nese Cabaroglu, *University of Cukurova, Turkey*
Pamela M. Denicolo, *University of Surrey, UK*
Nicola Simmons, *Brock University, Canada*

Founding Editor:

Michael Kompf† (Brock University, Canada)

Scope:

This series represents a forum for important issues that do and will affect how learning and teaching are thought about and practised. All educational venues and situations are undergoing change because of information and communications technology, globalization and paradigmatic shifts in determining what knowledge is valued. Our scope includes matters in primary, secondary and tertiary education as well as community-based informal circumstances. Important and significant differences between information and knowledge represent a departure from traditional educational offerings heightening the need for further and deeper understanding of the implications such opportunities have for influencing what happens in schools, colleges and universities around the globe. An inclusive approach helps attend to important current and future issues related to learners, teachers and the variety of cultures and venues in which educational efforts occur. We invite forward-looking contributions that reflect an international comparative perspective illustrating similarities and differences in situations, problems, solutions and outcomes.

Pedagogical Peculiarities

Conversations at the Edge of University Teaching and Learning

Edited by

Emma Medland
University of Surrey, UK

Richard Watermeyer
University of Bath, UK

Anesa Hosein
University of Surrey, UK

Ian M. Kinchin
University of Surrey, UK

and

Simon Lygo-Baker
University of Surrey, UK

BRILL
SENSE

LEIDEN | BOSTON

The Library of Congress Cataloging-in-Publication Data is available online at
http://catalog.loc.gov

ISBN: 978-94-6351-252-7 (paperback)
ISBN: 978-94-6351-253-4 (hardback)
ISBN: 978-94-6351-254-1 (e-book)

All chapters in this book have undergone peer review.

Cover illustration by Evie G.C. Medland (4 years old)

Copyright 2018 by Koninklijke Brill NV, Leiden, The Netherlands.

Koninklijke Brill NV incorporates the imprints Brill, Brill Hes & De Graaf, Brill Nijhoff, Brill Rodopi, Brill Sense and Hotei Publishing.

All rights reserved. No part of this publication may be reproduced, translated, stored in a retrieval system, or transmitted in any form or by any means, electronic, mechanical, photocopying, recording or otherwise, without prior written permission from the publisher.

Authorization to photocopy items for internal or personal use is granted by Koninklijke Brill NV provided that the appropriate fees are paid directly to The Copyright Clearance Center, 222 Rosewood Drive, Suite 910, Danvers, MA 01923, USA. Fees are subject to change.

This book is printed on acid-free paper and produced in a sustainable manner.

*To the memory of
Joanne Heywood*

TABLE OF CONTENTS

Preface		ix
1.	Pedagogical Peculiarities *Stephen D. Brookfield*	1
2.	Redefining Professionalism through an Examination of Personal and Social Values in Veterinary Teaching *Karen M. Young and Simon Lygo-Baker*	17
3.	"Messy and Precise": Peculiarities and Parallels between the Performing Arts and Higher Education *Emma Medland, Alison James and Niall Bailey*	33
4.	Research as Pedagogy in Academic Development: A Case Study *Ian M. Kinchin, Martyn Kingsbury and Stefan Yoshi Buhmann*	49
5.	The Vulnerability of a Small Discipline and Its Search for Appropriate Pedagogy: The Case of Medical Physics *Anesa Hosein and Jamie Harle*	69
6.	The Marketization of Pedagogy and the Problem of 'Competitive Accountability' *Richard Watermeyer and Michael Tomlinson*	87
7.	Strategic Pedagogic Management: Balancing Act or Symbiotic Relationship between Enhancement and Assurance *Gill Nicholls and Simon Lygo-Baker*	99
8.	Building an Agenda for Academic Development on the Peculiarity of University Teaching *Paul Ashwin*	113
About the Contributors		125

PREFACE

This book is published at a time when higher education is in a state of flux. Over the course of a decade we have seen the peculiar challenges of massification, internationalisation, and an increasingly diverse body of students and teachers. Higher education researchers like Rajani Naidoo (e.g. 2016) and Philip Altbach (e.g. 2016), point to how factors of globalisation and internationalisation have placed significant challenges to how the academic community responds to an ever diversifying student population. With an international, socially and culturally diverse student and teaching body, there emerges an array of requirements and challenges that need to be understood and addressed. These are grounded in the increased marketization and bureaucracy that characterises contemporary higher education. As a result, higher education has perhaps become more risk-averse as the student voice gains greater authority. Universities have become distracted by league tables and appear increasingly nervous of new forms of performance regulation that will label academics as excellent teachers, or not.

However, teaching is just one element of the professional role that characterises the traditional academic, the other substantive components of which are research and administration. Within this tripartite structure of the role, academics are seen to gravitate towards just one or other of these as a preferred activity, highlighting what Macfarlane (2011) refers to as the '*unbundling*' of the academic role. Consequently, talk centres on academics as effective teachers, or excellent researchers, or successful managers. Far less often it seems, do we think of academics as a coherent combination of all three. This is the consequence of an ideologically-informed values system in higher education that places research at the pinnacle of professional esteem and status, followed, arguably not too far behind by administration as another route to institutional power and authority. Lagging in third, lies teaching; rather less well thought of, though still seen as important. '*Teacher-bashing*' has been recognised as a '*popular sport*' for some time (Palmer, 1998: 3), being fuelled by the pressures created by the current consumerist view of higher education. Nevertheless, teaching is also a form of activity from which, ironically, the university in many national contexts achieves its major form of funding and, therefore, sustainability.

In an attempt to create greater balance between research and teaching, a spotlight on teaching excellence in higher education has resulted in the proliferation of academic developers recruited by universities to support and encourage the pedagogical enhancement of academic staff (Gibbs, 2013). This has been accompanied by the recognition and reward of teaching excellence through the award of fellowship by professional bodies, such as the UK's Higher Education Academy (HEA), which provides benchmark accreditation that has increasingly become a requirement of academic appointment. However, a spotlight on teaching excellence implies that there is a single ultimate target to reach for, which raises significant questions as to what is understood by teaching quality in a sector that is renowned and revered for its autonomy and diversity.

Pedagogical Peculiarities

Set within this context are higher education institutions that are *peculiar* places of teaching and learning. This peculiarity emerges from the idiosyncrasies that are inherent in the way higher education is both conceptualised and organised. The peculiarity of pedagogy in higher education is apparent in the way different disciplines are characterised by different kinds of spaces and different approaches to teaching and learning, or signature pedagogies as Shulman (2006) describes them. For instance, a pedagogy of performance followed in the training of actors or singers in post-compulsory settings is very different from the kinds of pedagogy we tend to associate with teaching and learning in the social sciences, which in turn differ from the kinds of pedagogy witnessed in teaching hospitals. The peculiarity of pedagogy also lives within the array of seeming contradictions between espoused and enacted practices. For example, whilst outwardly espousing innovation and creativity, contemporary higher education may be found largely to enact this in a manner that conforms to homogenous and conservative norms of practice.

It is important to note that we think of peculiarities not in a pejorative, but in a celebratory sense. However, some of these peculiarities can lead to schisms within the traditional academic identity, particularly within research-intensive institutions. Here, the keystones of the role demand different approaches to practice where, as we have seen, pedagogic practice is often perceived to be the poorer partner of research, leading to teaching that can be described as 'research-drained' (Hosein, 2017). It is also important that we unpack our own interpretation of pedagogy. This we take as something that not only signposts the relationship that underpins the transmission and co-creation of knowledge, but a knowledge-based relationship that catalyses social, cultural, political and economic transformations. We thus think of pedagogy as that which underpins what it is, not only to be a teacher, but also a researcher and even a manager. Therefore, pedagogical peculiarity, for us, is recognition of the way in which higher education is itself a unique opportunity for immersion in multiple and diverse relationships of and with knowledge. These relationships are then enacted through a varied range of practices, ideologies and aspirations concerning how to, where to, and with whom to teach. And yet this is an aspect of the higher education discourse that struggles to find a voice due, in part, to 'a profession that fears the personal and seeks safety in the technical, the distant, the abstract' (Palmer, 1998: 12).

In response to this fear of the personal, we have chosen to adopt a less conventional, conversational approach (Gall et al., 2003) to critical inquiry that is

PREFACE

arranged as a series of what we term '*deliberative dialogues*'. These dialogues will take place between experts in pedagogy and academics working within specific disciplinary and institutional contexts. It will respond to existing empirical and conceptual '*blank-spots*' related to how pedagogical development is perceived, experienced and responded to by academics across the disciplines. In so doing, it will stimulate critical awareness of the influence of pedagogical development on academic tribes and territories (Becher & Trowler, 2001). This will be achieved through a consideration of the key challenges faced and workarounds developed in response. It is intended to cater for broad and deep reflection, exploration, discovery and interrogation of the *peculiarities* and of their contexts. Through this approach, we hope to illuminate the processes undertaken by academics in developing their academic practice and pedagogic knowledge-base, and will provide a necessary and currently missing critique of the *peculiarity* of teaching practice and the idealisation of teaching excellence in higher education (as opposed to enhancement). In essence, we intend to explore what it means to be a contemporary academic.

This book attempts to interrogate how academics in a range of contemporary higher education settings seek to understand the implications, issues and impacts associated with their work in current, and often challenging, contexts. In so doing, the authors will unpack the pedagogical *peculiarities* characterising their university teaching cultures. This will be achieved through an exploration of the relationship between identity on an individual, disciplinary and institutional level. Identity is of particular significance as it underpins who we are, and what we do as practitioners. As Palmer (1998: 10) notes:

> good teaching cannot be reduced to technique; good teaching comes from the identity and integrity of the teacher…good teachers share one trait: a strong sense of personal identity infuses their work.

Ultimately the book's distinctiveness is its articulation of different pedagogical identities. These emanate from, and are characterised by different teaching and learning environments – across different institutions and sectors. As such, the major contribution of *Pedagogical Peculiarities* lies in the development of a discourse of pedagogy in higher education, comprised of multiple contexts. This serves to highlight the current contexts and challenges across higher education as they relate and respond to ideology, values, policy and changes in the organisation of the sector.

And so we begin this book by first reflecting on what it is to enact a teaching role. Where is the role situated? Is it at least on the surface, lower down a pecking order of priorities within an academic role? Is it seen as being an obstacle that impedes the fulfilment of other aspects of the academic role? We argue that self-scrutiny of our professional identities will serve to critique the reductionist notions of what a university education and even what the university is for (Collini, 2012). It will also serve to extend our understanding of the complexity and messiness of the academic role, particularly as it is framed by pedagogy. As a result, each chapter of

xi

PREFACE

this book serves to illuminate a variety of the tensions that arise between different stakeholders (e.g. students, staff, senior management), levels (e.g. societal, sectorial, institutional, disciplinary and individual), and disciplines/fields (e.g. veterinary medicine, performing arts, medical physics). Underpinning and, indeed potentially fuelling such tensions, are the personal and collective values that inform individual, disciplinary and institutional identity. However, in spite of the tensions, challenges and areas of contestation that each chapter raises, there is also a collective call for reciprocal relationships to be established through a more holistic approach to academic practice that is informed and guided by dialogue.

OVERVIEW OF BOOK STRUCTURE

As outlined above, a theme running through this volume focuses on academics seeking to understand their work in current (and challenging) contexts, in relation to their pedagogical identities at three key levels:

i. Individual level;
ii. Disciplinary level, and;
iii. Institutional level.

As a result, in addition to the introductory (chapter 1) and concluding (chapter 8) chapters, *Pedagogical Peculiarities* is divided into three sections:

a. Identity as it relates to teaching (chapters 2 and 3);
b. Identity as it relates to the discipline (chapters 4 and 5), and;
c. Identity as it relates to the institution (chapters 6 and 7).

In chapter 1, Brookfield focuses on two peculiarities of higher education: ideological control, and contextuality. The first peculiarity draws attention to the ideological control that pervades higher education in the form of instrumentalism. The second highlights the constant presence of contextuality in that the illusion of pedagogic independence is broken down when acknowledging the influence of the wider context (i.e. institutional, political, societal etc.) on ones pedagogic practices. These peculiarities intersect within the generally unacknowledged meta-peculiarity of higher education pedagogy – its emotional nature. As Brookfield notes, 'Living with the fiction of controllability and emotional evenness is impossible when you're constantly having to make adjustments seemingly "on the fly"'. Thus highlighting the inherently unpredictable nature of teaching and learning and need for a revival of rebellious subjectivity.

a. Identity as it relates to teaching

In their chapter that focuses on the influence of personal values on professional practice and how these relate to the concept of professionalism, Young and Lygo-Baker consider the interplay between the individual and the group(s) encountered

PREFACE

over a career in the formation of identity. Within chapter 2, the authors reflect upon how identity and professionalism are linked. As Brookfield calls for in chapter 1, Young and Lygo-Baker argue for a less instrumental approach to how professionalism is conceived. This may be achieved through an exploration of how personal values influence identity, and an acknowledgement of the benefits (and challenges) of pluralism in the learning and teaching environment. The authors point out that it is only through a broadening of what is encompassed by the concept of professionalism, through the examination of the interaction between personal and collective values that practitioners can connect espoused with enacted practice and evolve as teachers. Thereby supporting students from subject expertise (i.e. competency) to expert practice, as discussed in chapter 4.

In chapter 3, Medland, James and Bailey, explore the competing pressures of personal versus social identity within the context of the performing arts. They consider the misalignments that can emerge between identity, aspirations and the values of the institution, discipline and individual. Much of these tensions are grounded within the market-driven instrumentalist ideology that pervades higher education (as discussed in chapters 1 and 6), resulting in contestation between an individual's personal and social identity and values. Such tensions require individuals to explicitly explore the interaction between the two sets of values and, at times, to compromise. Such compromise can been seen as an encroachment on academic freedom and can result in divergent behaviours: it can force individuals into viewing the role of practitioner and educator as distinct and therefore in competition (as discussed by Nicholls and Lygo-Baker in chapter 7), or it can encourage individuals to revert back to their central point of reference (i.e. professional identity) which can lead to a stalemate. One means of addressing this impasse is through the adoption of a more collective approach to development. For an institution to support a more symbiotic interaction between personal and social identity, a greater focus on quality enhancement towards a more flexible approach to quality assurance that embraces the nuances of different subject areas, may be worthwhile and is supported by Nicholls and Lygo-Baker in chapter 7. Whilst examination of the values underpinning our pedagogic practice can support this from the individual perspective (as considered by Young and Lygo-Baker in chapter 2), thereby becoming less susceptible to the pedagogic frailty identified by Kinchin et al. in chapter 4.

b. Identity as it relates to the discipline

Kinchin, Kingsbury and Buhmann, in chapter 4, reflect upon the relationship between research and teaching within an academic development programme. Through their experiences of the programme, the authors reflect upon the pedagogical abilities that underpin the pathway between subject expertise and expert practice, and the need for academics to see pedagogy as a central feature of their disciplinary structure. In order to enhance the relationship between academic development and the disciplines, Kinchin et al. highlight the need to view research as pedagogy, thus supporting

PREFACE

academics to embrace a more scholarly approach to the pedagogy underpinning academic practice, and highlighting the potentially influential role of the external examiner within this process. Key to the enactment of research as pedagogy is the concepts of authenticity, prestige, and an ability to critically reflect upon practice. However, the perpetuation of separating research and teaching may contribute to the development of pedagogic frailty within an institution.

Hosein and Harle, in chapter 5, reflect upon the pedagogical vulnerability of a small interdisciplinary sub-discipline, Medical Physics, and the factors that may affect the implementation of an appropriate pedagogy. The authors explore the key challenges that impact Medical Physics and the disciplinary fracturing that has emerged based on the divergent pedagogic approaches of the two main post-graduation vocational applications (i.e. practice versus theory and research). This pedagogic disciplinary fracturing between institutions may cause conflict regarding which is the most appropriate pedagogical approach. Rivalry, nepotism and vulnerability, can all serve to strangle pedagogic innovation in favour of the status quo, as highlighted in chapter 7 by Nicholls and Lygo-Baker. Hosein and Harle, therefore, call for a more holistic approach to pedagogy (as argued for in relation to research and teaching in chapter 4, and quality assurance and quality enhancement in chapter 7), a community of practice that gives voice to and engages in dialogue with all stakeholders and, as Nicholls and Lygo-Baker advocate, that places students at the heart of the search for an appropriate pedagogy.

c. Identity as it relates to the institution

In their chapter that focuses on the influence of competitive accountability within the broader higher education context, Watermeyer and Tomlinson, as in chapter 1, dissect the influence of the marketization of pedagogy whilst acknowledging the influence of the national and global economy, and government. In an era of increasing public scrutiny, the authors of chapter 6 consider how this wider context can serve to reinforce the artificial separation of research and teaching (as considered by Kinchin et al. in chapter 4), and how the competitive accountability colouring higher education can conflict with personal identity, praxis and priorities (as discussed by Young and Lygo-Baker, in chapter 2). The subsequent cult of administration enforcing a performative audit culture can result in the destabilisation of identity caused by a conflict between personal and collective values, as unpacked by Medland et al. in chapter 3. Watermeyer and Tomlinson proceed to argue that higher education's audit society deincentivises pedagogical development in favour of pedagogical conservatism, as discussed by Kinchin et al., and erodes trust (as considered by Young and Lygo-Baker in chapter 2) in favour of continuous performance evaluations. In response to these challenges, the authors seek to '*free pedagogy from its coupling with performance*', by listening to the critical demands of the student (as concluded by Nicholls and Lygo-Baker in chapter 7). And, as

Young and Lygo-Baker contest, to transform the focus from a competitive to a moral imperative.

In chapter 7, Nicholls and Lygo-Baker focus on the architecture of the higher education landscape by exploring the tensions emerging between pedagogical experimentation and resistance to change within a higher education framework in flux. Central to this focus sits the relationship between quality assurance and quality enhancement, as discussed in chapters 3 (Medland et al.) and 4 (Kinchin et al.). According to the authors, at the heart of the interplay between quality assurance and enhancement, lies the student and their relationship to other stakeholders (e.g. staff, the institution), particularly with regard to their potential to influence both strands. Where perceived conflicts emerge between legislative interpretation and enhancement for instance, this can remove the centrality of the student in favour of maintaining the status quo, and lead to unnecessary perceived juxtapositions between quality assurance and enhancement. Nicholls and Lygo-Baker go on to highlight the influential nature of ones values and fundamentality of staying true to these whilst acknowledging the importance of locating workarounds that aim towards the synthesis of quality assurance and enhancement. However, this can result in retrenching into ones disciplinary boundaries due to perceptions of threats to the identity of the person or group, as seen in Medland et al.'s chapter 3, thus highlighting the importance of trust as considered by Young and Lygo-Baker (chapter 2) and Watermeyer and Tomlinson (chapter 6). As a result, the authors emphasise the importance of celebrating disciplinary differences within the concept of professionalising pedagogic practice and encouraging a symbiotic relationship between quality assurance and enhancement so that a meaningful dialogue is created and sustained between stakeholders (e.g. students, staff, senior management etc.).

Finally, in the concluding chapter of the book (chapter 8), Ashwin shifts the focus from teaching in higher education to the peculiar nature of academic development. In pursuing the question of what is distinctive about university teaching (as opposed to other levels of education) the author identifies the three forms of knowledge (knowledge-as-research; knowledge-as-curriculum, and; knowledge-as-student-understanding) that are produced within a single institution. In considering this peculiar feature of university teaching as a framework for reflecting upon the preceding chapters, Ashwin examines seven tensions that have important implications for how we understand the nature of academic development and its relationship to the enhancement of teaching and learning at an institutional and sector-wide level. As considered in the previous chapters, the seven tensions identified by the author explore what it is to be a contemporary academic, the contestation between enhancement and excellence and the crucial role that academic development plays in supporting the development of less conformist approaches to university teaching. In so doing, Ashwin concludes *Pedagogical Peculiarities* by seeking to develop a coherent, holistic and challenging agenda for the future of academic development.

REFERENCES

Altbach, P. G. (2016). *Global perspectives on higher education.* Baltimore, MD: Johns Hopkins University Press.
Becher, T., & Trowler, P. (2001). *Academic tribes and territories: Intellectual enquiry and the culture of disciplines.* Buckingham: SRHE and Open University Press.
Collini, S. (2012). *What are universities for?* London: Penguin.
Hosein, A. (2017). Pedagogic frailty and the research-teaching nexus. In I. M. Kinchin & N. E. Winstone (Eds.), *Pedagogic frailty and resilience in the university.* Rotterdam: Sense Publishers.
Gall, M. D., Gall, J. P., & Borg, W. R. (2003). *Educational research: An introduction* (7th ed.). Boston, MA: Allyn & Bacon Publications.
Gibbs, G. (2013) Reflections on the changing nature of educational development. *International Journal for Academic Development, 18*(1): 4–14.
Macfarlane, B. (2011). The morphing of academic practice: Unbundling and the rise of the para-academic. *Higher Education Quarterly, 65*(1), 59–73.
Naidoo, R. (2016). The competition fetish in higher education: Varieties, animators and consequences. *British Journal of Sociology of Education, 37*(1), 1–10.
Palmer, P. (1998). *The courage to teach.* San Francisco, CA: Jossey-Bass.
Shulman, L. S. (2006). Signature pedagogies in the professions. *Daedalus, 134*(3), 52–59.

STEPHEN D. BROOKFIELD

1. PEDAGOGICAL PECULIARITIES

AN INTRODUCTION

The particular peculiarity of teaching smashed into my consciousness with unassailable force in September 1970. I'd been employed as a part-time teacher of 'Liberal Studies' at Lewisham and Eltham College of Further Education in south east London. Several dramatic events happened in my first two days of teaching, the most memorable of which was when an inter-racial fist fight broke out in one of my classes between an English boy and a Caribbean boy. I was, of course, completely clueless about what to do. Somehow I got through the lesson relatively unscathed without police or even other teachers showing up in class. But as I rode back to my shared bedsit that night I remember asking myself 'how do people do this for a living?'

The longer I taught the more I realized that this incident revealed a fundamental peculiarity of life in higher education. Colleges and universities are organized on an assumption that is profoundly distorted; the assumption that teaching and learning are primarily cognitive phenomena that can therefore be rationally organized. Programs are designed, curricula are developed, measures of assessment are implemented and teaching activities are planned, all premised on the idea that learning occurs in a logically sequenced way. Classroom and homework exercises are structured to take students from the simple to the complex, the introductory to the intermediate and advanced and from uncritical assimilation to critical analysis. The organizing vision is of learners gradually internalizing skills and knowledge as they advance along a measurable continuum of progress. Who benefits from this vision? And where does a racially motivated fist fight fit into this neat picture?

This highly rational vision of learning works for the good of funding institutions and administrators, not learners. It assumes that learning proceeds forward in a linear manner without any plateaus or fall backs. It also assumes that learning is experienced in roughly the same way by all those enrolled in any particular degree. And, of course, it assumes that learning is a matter of cognition, of developing thoughtful reasoning in which powers of analysis, logic and appraisal become refined over time. In perhaps the biggest peculiarity of all, higher education completely ignores the emotional underpinning to so much learning and teaching. The triumph of the instrumentalist view of higher education is to make college and university practices all a matter of informational and pedagogic inputs and pre-identified learning outcomes. Learning thus becomes commodified in terms of attainment and testing, with comparisons supposedly being able to be drawn across and between scores on standardized tests. This allows for the full paraphernalia of league tables, institutional rankings and the grading of teachers on a spuriously valid axis of '*competence*'.

The absence in standardized assessment measures of any recognition of the powerful role that emotions play in learning and teaching is probably not surprising given their inherent volatility. Emotions explode the pretence of controllability. When that fight broke out in my first week of college teaching I knew that I was not controlling anything. Obviously, I couldn't control the emotional lives of the students involved and nor could I control the responses of other members of the class. But just as importantly for me I couldn't control my own emotions. Although that day happened in September 1970 I can still recall the fear and panic that washed over me that morning as I saw the fragile vision of college teaching as civil but critical dialogue get smashed into pieces. I was clueless and alone, fearful that a classroom riot was about to break out and deeply embarrassed by my inability of knowing how to respond.

For the rest of that first year of part-time teaching my existence was completely dominated by the fear of losing control. I only taught on Thursday and Friday each week but those two days were the experiential Mount Kilimanjaro towering over the Great Plains of my everyday existence from Saturday to Wednesday. My time out of the classroom was consumed either by preparing myself for the impostorship I knew I would feel as soon as I entered the college premises, or by trying to keep my self-laceration at bay as I reflected on the failure I had been. I can't really remember any of the exercises or activities I employed during that year, but I can bring that state of fearful panic to mind in an instant.

In this chapter I want to examine two particular pedagogic peculiarities, both of which are woven throughout the chapters in this book. The first peculiarity is the ideologically grounded nature of pedagogy. I contend that as we are engaging in the seemingly neutral business of teaching our subject's content many of us are caught in ideological contradictions that produce frustration, alienation and sadness. Spending your life trying to work in a way that feels student-centred, democratic or radical, all the while being constrained and compromised by politically inspired structural reforms is bound to take its emotional toll.

The second peculiarity – the contextuality of practice – explores how plans, predictions and possibilities developed in tranquillity become transformed into something completely different when executed in a real life setting. Muddling through particularity and uncertainty is the ontology of college teaching. An exercise that worked wonderfully well with a group last week falls dismally flat with another group this week. A well-rehearsed activity spirals out of control because of an unanticipated question that's been raised or a particular student's reaction. Living with the fiction of controllability and emotional evenness is impossible when you constantly have to make adjustments seemingly '*on the fly*'.

THE IDEOLOGICAL NATURE OF PEDAGOGY; ALONE WHILST NEVER ALONE

This first peculiarity focuses on the way in which classroom events are shaped by forces and structures in the world outside. My discussion of this peculiarity is framed within the perspective of the body of work known as critical social theory (Brookfield, 2005). One of my early assumptions as a teacher was that the classroom was a sort of fiefdom in which I was the Lord of the Manor able to control what happened within my domain. I have always taught with the classroom door shut, even when my employing organization has preferred an open door policy. This is because I'd regarded the classroom as *my* space, an arena in which I could do what I wanted. My classroom door was closed because I didn't want the outside world intruding while I was doing my own pedagogic thing in the little world I was creating.

The illusory nature of this assumption of pedagogic independence was made apparent in the first couple of weeks of my career. My students were all apprentices learning electrical, plumbing, heating and secretarial trades and once word got back to their employers that they were expected to spend an hour of their day release in '*Liberal Studies*' all hell broke loose. My students told me in the second or third week of term that their employers had flatly informed them that the hour spent with me was totally unnecessary and that they should not be wasting their time showing up to my class. So a further assumption I'd held – that college students were there because they wanted to learn – was dismantled.

Over the years this peculiarity has become a central feature of my reality. I am alone while never being alone. By this I mean that I am physically alone in the classroom in the sense that I am usually teaching solo, either face-to-face or online. Yet my actions are always embedded in a web of networks that shape my decisions. So my room is symbolically stacked with holographic images of the multiple stakeholders whose agendas and priorities influence very directly the micro-decisions I constantly make as a teacher. About a decade into my career Margaret Thatcher was one of these holograms and my refusal to pay attention to her meant I was fired in 1981 at the beginning of her austerity regime. Provosts, Presidents, heads of department and Boards of Trustees members are always in the room but so also are state legislators, local council members, members of congress, senators and the President of the United States. Prominent alumni whose generous financial donations have funded the buildings in which I work are there along with a range of media figures, bloggers and commentators whose ranting's frame the climate of opinion surrounding the proper purpose and functioning of higher education. There are corporate CEO's whose agendas and lobbying change national budgetary priorities and determine what's left for education. And, always lurking in the background is the presence of the accreditation agencies that bestow credibility on my organization.

The external boards that accredited the diplomas and certification my students were pursuing back in 1970 required that students receive the one hour of '*Liberal Studies*' instruction I was hired to provide. But, as already mentioned, the employers who subsidized the students' attendance opposed this. When I worked in community adult education I was encouraged to develop courses and workshops that were creative and flexible, yet my Local Education Authority (LEA) needed these to be financially stable. So if I ran a weekend institute on, say, '*Living in Communes*', this would have to be balanced by a weekly Yoga class to ensure that my enrolment numbers looked good. In my first American University post I was told by the President that it didn't matter how much I published or how good the reviews of my teaching were, I needed to bring in 20–25 new postgraduate students a year so that their tuition fees could fund my line.

A specific example of how these holograms directly affect my pedagogy has been repeated four times in three different institutions. In each of these universities I taught in doctoral programmes in which team-teaching was the norm. Each of these programmes had been approved with the understanding that team-teaching was the preferred pedagogy for doctoral level work. The benefits of team-teaching have been well documented (Eisen & Tisdell, 2000; Plank, 2011). A team of professors can model both collaboration and critique, and demonstrate in a vividly personal way the reality that multiple viewpoints usually exist around issues of the moment in any disciplinary field. A team can model striving for intersubjective understanding – seeing an issue through colleagues' eyes – by asking questions that sought to understand a contrary point of view. They can show what respectful disagreement looks like. In a team taught course students can see examples of people changing their minds as they're convinced by a better argument or more persuasive evidence, and of how being open to critique is essential to intellectual development.

In these three different postgraduate programmes team-teaching was deliberately chosen as the preferred model of instruction to help students learn. Classroom exercises were developed, curriculum was planned and assessment was designed all to be an analogue of the team-teaching approach adopted by faculty. So there was a heavy emphasis on group projects, on student-led '*teach-ins*', even the adoption of a new doctoral dissertation format that allowed final theses to be written collaboratively by teams of students. Yet, in all three of these university doctorates the team teaching model was eventually abandoned solely for budgetary reasons. Students had consistently evaluated the team-teaching approach as a highlight of these programmes and the lecturers and professors remained completely committed to the method. But, as endowments dropped, enrolments declined, competitors priced their doctorates more cheaply, and trustees hired new institutional leaders to '*clean house*', '*get rid of dead wood*' and '*forge a path for the future*', the administrators of these programmes were all told that team-teaching was to be abandoned. No matter that the whole doctoral student experience had been deliberately designed around this pedagogy, it was now considered just too expensive.

In the first two decades of the twenty first century, higher education (at least in the three countries in which I've worked – the United Kingdom, Canada, and the USA) is ideologically determined by the acceptance of the twin ideologies of capitalism and bureaucratic rationality. This is why an understanding of the body of work of critical social theory (Browne, 2017) becomes necessary for us to understand the daily pedagogic decisions we make. Critical theory explores how blatantly unequal systems stay in place with minimal challenge to their legitimacy. Consent is secured through the dissemination of dominant ideology. Basically, if people can be persuaded to accept the idea that things are organized the way they are for the ultimate good of all, and that the bad things that happen (being fired, hospitals, post offices and schools closing) are as uncontrollable as the onset of a hurricane or snow storm, then the system remains intact.

Abandoning team-teaching as the primary pedagogy in doctorates described was linked directly to external political events. First was the financial collapse of 2008 that wiped out many university endowments, caused potential students to lose jobs and be unable to afford tuition, and meant that enormous state resources had to be channelled to propping up the banks, insurance companies and financial houses that were '*too big to fail*'. Second was the growth of Indian, Chinese and South East Asian economies that led to capital moving overseas and jobs being lost in the USA. Third was the urging of business and opinion leaders that higher education should promote the STEM (science, technology, engineering and mathematics) disciplines in order that the US be able to compete more effectively in the global marketplace by inventing new products and production processes. Along with this went the declared need to prepare students for professional roles in managing the new information and service (rather than manufacturing) economy.

The matter of fact acceptance of the ideology of unfettered capitalism framed all these events. After the financial collapse the response of the media, political elites and opinion-maker class was that capitalism was to be preserved at all costs. So it's no surprise that the doctorates in adult education that I helped create were prime targets for gutting as universities moved to funding STEM schools and departments and as schools of law, entrepreneurship and business were expanded. Since having two or three lecturers teach one course was much costlier than having only one person in charge, it was decreed that team teaching cease. So the removal of team teaching from these programmes can thus be traced directly back to the actions of the major players in the 2008 financial collapse. To me there can't be a clearer example of how the minutiae of practice is always to some extent determined by broader political events.

As mentioned earlier working within an ideologically framed higher education system that has become increasingly tied to the needs of capitalism puts many teachers in an emotionally dissonant situation. So many of us go into university teaching because we love our subjects and want to share the primary joy of intellectual discovery that we experienced as novice learners. We want '*to turn our students on*' to the joys of engineering, theology, history, mathematics or sociology so that they feel the excitement we enjoyed as we saw things come together, encounter new ideas or be stimulated by an uncomfortable critique. We also want to teach authentically in a way that reflects who we are as people with enthusiasms, passions and frailties. We don't want always to have to be the '*expert*' who constantly enforces rules as norms; rather, we wish to be a collaborative co-learner participating in a common intellectual quest.

But this desire to work in an authentic way is in constant contradiction to the ideological nature of higher education. I have already talked about the way in which capitalism frames educational practices, so let me turn now to another associated ideological component – bureaucratic rationality. Bureaucratic rationality is the organizing principle that flows from the ethic of capitalism. Just as manufacturing is organized most profitably based on the division of labour, so bureaucratic rationality posits that organizations like colleges and universities work most effectively when teaching and learning is divided into discrete units. Disciplinary divides function on the principle that knowledge can be compartmentalized; theology over here and philosophy over there, as if each occupies its own epistemological universe. Within disciplines knowledge is chunked into components and instruction is similarly chunked into temporal blocks; you will learn this topic from 11.00 a.m.–11.55 a.m. each Tuesday and Thursday.

Two classics of critical theory – *Eclipse of Reason* (Horkheimer, 1974) and *Dialectic of Enlightenment* (Horkheimer & Adorno, 1972) – examine the ways in which bureaucratic rationality has led to thought and reasoning becoming instrumentalised. In *Eclipse of Reason* (1974) Horkheimer argues that the capacity to reason (surely a central concern of anyone working in higher education) has been dominated by the shift to an instrumental kind of reason, one 'essentially concerned with means and ends, with the adequacy of procedures for purposes more or less taken for granted and supposedly self-explanatory' (p. 3). When reason is instrumentalised it is made subservient to practical utilitarian ends. Diverting reason from the study of universal questions, and attaching it to the resolution of short term practical problems, also serves to maintain the current political and economic order.

Instrumental reasoning displays a dominance of means-end thinking whereby reason is applied to solve problems of how to attain certain short-term social and economic objectives. Its application to exploring abstract universals such as justice, equality and tolerance becomes viewed as impractical and unrealistic, irrelevant to the social project of retaining a competitive edge in global capitalism. This is the triumph of what Herbert Marcuse (1964) called one dimensional thought. One dimensional thought is instrumental thought focused on how to make the current system work better and perform more effectively. When people think this way they start to conceive of the range of possibilities open to them in life within a framework predefined by the existing order. People assume that all is for the best in society, that things are arranged the way they are for a good reason, and that the current system works for the benefit of all. In this system philosophical thought, even of an apparently critical kind, serves only to keep the system going.

The higher education factory produces artefacts and commodities – papers, projects, test results, theses and dissertations – that are assigned value both within the institution and in the wider marketplace. Within the institution points and grades are awarded to student work that accumulate over time into a grade point average or some other cumulative marker of value. These markers of value become conflated with students' self-image so that receiving anything less than an 'A' becomes a personal tragedy. Students negotiate for grades with teachers to develop their personal portfolios of accomplishment that are then presented to future employers or to secure entry into postgraduate programmes. Drawing on Marx (1961) this is the commodification of learning; the turning of the creative labour of learning into an artefact assigned an external value. The use value of the labour (its meaning and utility for the student) is far overshadowed by its exchange value (the better jobs or entry into programmes of further study it is traded for).

It's also clear that students, at least in the USA where I work, enter into an economic calculation when deciding where and what to study. Regarding the location of study, I have been a professor at two elite Ivy League universities (Columbia and Harvard) and at each one I was struck by the fact that the tuition students paid for their degrees and diplomas was several times higher than that of many surrounding universities. When I asked students why they didn't get their Bachelor's, Master's or doctorate at a much less expensive institution they told me overwhelmingly that they were prepared to pay an outrageous amount of money because a degree from an Ivy League institution was worth so much more in the market place and in terms of prestige and status. Students had assigned a value to their degrees assuming that these could be traded for better paying and higher status jobs.

The ideology of bureaucratic rationality has a profound impact on the lives of teachers who regard themselves working within progressive, radical or humanistic traditions, all of which emphasize student-centeredness, creativity and the creation of democratic classrooms. Bureaucratic rationality supports a system set up to make realizing those traditions very difficult and trying to subvert from within carries with it the promise of a life of frustration and alienation. This reality is implicit in Simon Lygo-Baker and Karen Young's discussion in chapter 2 of the way that unquestioned disciplinary boundaries and identities preclude a complex, interdisciplinary analysis of knowledge. Anesa Hosein and Jamie Harle's commentary in chapter 5 on how external regulators and accreditation bodies enforce compliance also illustrates the difficulties of working in creative ways.

Bureaucratic rationality underlies the accountability discourse examined by Emma Medland, Alison James and Niall Bailey in chapter 3 and aspects of university management by Gill Nicholls and Simon Lygo-Baker in chapter 7. Accountability makes sense only if you believe a valid and reliable measure of achievement can be laid over the reality of the complexities of learning that exist in a single class, let alone across multiple disciplines and institutions. Exercising the kind of creativity in teaching methods and forms of assessment explored by Richard Watermeyer and Michael Tomlinson in chapter 6 becomes almost impossible if you work in a system that commodifies learning, divides it into discrete disciplines and instructional units, and overlays learning with the temporal necessity of being forced to complete specified objectives and attain declared outcomes by a certain calendar date. Disciplinary divides are further compounded by the argument that signature pedagogies – approaches to teaching that are unique to a particular discipline – prevent any transfer of ideas or practices across departments and divisions (Gurung, Chick, & Haynie, 2009; Chick, Haynie, & Gurung, 2012). Ian M. Kinchin, Martyn Kingsbury and Stefan Yoshi Buhmann also emphasize in chapter 4 the peculiarity, not to say idiocy, of assuming that the different rhythms of teaching and research can be compressed into a unitary time frame.

One final matter needs addressing in this discussion of the first peculiarity and that is aesthetics and play. In two other classics of critical theory – *An Essay on Liberation* (1969) and *The Aesthetic Dimension* (1978) – Herbert Marcuse developed a theory of critical learning that has direct implications for the issues examined in more detail in the chapters ahead. Essentially Marcuse argued that a crucial dynamic in learning to think critically was exposing students to some kind of unmediated aesthetic engagement. In order to free people from the instrumental reasoning so dominant in one dimensional thought, they needed to experience a powerfully estranging experience that would shatter their normal ways of thinking, seeing and believing. This was the function of art, broadly defined as aesthetic engagements (poetry, films, realistic and abstract art, music, plays, novels and so on). Tasting a new form of experience is inherently revolutionary according to Marcuse and the power to initiate this is 'the critical, negating function of art' (Marcuse, 1978, p. 7). Art can induce 'the transcendence of immediate reality' which 'shatters the reified objectivity of established social relations and opens a new dimension of experience: rebirth of the rebellious subjectivity' (ibid.).

Marcuse is careful to recognize that 'art cannot change the world' (1978, p. 32) though he does believe that 'it can contribute to changing the consciousness and drives of the men and women who could change the world' (ibid.). Art represents only 'the promise of liberation' (1978, p. 46) not its actuality, and 'clearly, the fulfilment of this promise is not within the domain of art' (ibid.). What art does offer us, however, is a chance of breaking with the familiar, of inducing in us an awareness of other ways of being in the world. Art 'opens the established reality to another dimension; that of possible liberation' (1972, p. 87). If radical political practice is focused on creating 'a world different from and contrary to the established universe of discourse and behaviour' (1969, p. 73) then art is one important prompt to this state of difference. Working to create a free society therefore 'involves a break with the familiar, the routine ways of seeing, hearing, feeling, understanding things so that the organism may become receptive to the potential forms of a non-aggressive, non-exploitative world' (1969, p. 6).

When we submit to the aesthetic power of a work of art we immerse ourselves in an experience in which different rules are present. There is a tyranny of form and structure present, 'a necessity which demands that no line, no sound could be replaced' (1978, p. 42). Because the rules of creative, artistic necessity are radically different from those governing social and economic necessity, works of art that adhere to these rules induce an estrangement from contemporary life. In this way 'art breaks open a dimension inaccessible to other experiences, a dimension in which human beings, nature, and things no longer stand under the law of the established reality principle' (1978, p. 72). The rules that make for effective art (effectiveness being defined as the capacity to induce an altered consciousness) are quite separate from the rules that make for effective adult education practice, to take one example. Art 'has its own language and illuminates reality only through this other language' (p. 22).

Marcuse's theory of aesthetics seems to speak most directly to the issues regarding the performing arts discussed in chapter 3 by Emma Medland, Alison James and Niall Bailey. However, the logic of Marcuse's argument is really discipline-free. If artistic engagement is an element of critical thinking that helps people think out of the box, avoid disciplinary groupthink and escape the dominance of disciplinary paradigms then encouraging students to engage with the arts is just as crucial for Simon Lygo-Baker and Karen Young's description of veterinary pedagogy in chapter 2 and to the small disciplines examined in chapter 5 by Anesa Hosein and Jamie Harle. Furthermore, the standardized licensing and accreditation measures discussed by Richard Watermeyer and Michael Tomlinson in chapter 6 have little or no place for assessing the effectiveness of the aesthetic engagements argued by Marcuse as necessary to critical thought. This is because the encounters with art that Marcuse urges must be separate from any kind of educational supervision or monitoring.

For people to function as autonomous critical thinkers they must be able to remove themselves from the day to day reality of the surrounding culture. Immersion in artistic experience is one way to induce an estrangement from the rhythms of normal life, but it must be solitary. Experiencing art communally at a gallery, theatre, poetry reading or concert is, Marcuse argues, inherently conservative. Our responses to the art concerned are pre-conditioned by our awareness of the presence of others and by the mediator's (the docent, music appreciation teacher, or headphones guide) effort to explain the art and place it in its historical context. But when someone experiences a deeply personal, completely private reaction to a work of art, she 'enters another dimension of existence' (1978, p. 4); the dimension of inwardness, of liberating subjectivity. Such subjectivity is liberating because we are moved by primal aesthetic and creative impulses, not the dictates of majority opinion or common sense criteria of beauty.

It would be impossible to compare multiple unsupervised student engagements with art using the language of accountability described in chapter 6. The whole point of the aesthetic experience in Marcuse's view is that it is unaccountable. There should be no attempt to compare artistic engagements to a norm or to demonstrate their societal utility. On the contrary, aesthetics is designed to shatter the notion of accountability and broader utility by replacing it with a powerful and sensual immediacy. If there is any merit to Marcuse's theory of aesthetics, then a basic contradiction exists between teaching students to think critically (the declared purpose of higher education) and competitive accountability. In order to think critically you must have an uncontrolled, unsupervised immersion in a powerful artistic experience that should be completely unaccountable or controlled. And this must happen individually with no formal curriculum or objectives in place that allow for comparisons to be made.

THE CLEANSING OF CONTEXTUALITY

Institutional conceptions of teaching are grounded in the notion of controllability. The assumption is that how and what students learn can be controlled by setting standardized learning objectives and outcomes, taking students through the same carefully sequenced curricula, administering standardized tests at the same points in a curricular sequence, and using common measures of assessment. Doing these things will allow comparisons to be made across multiple classrooms and institutions.

This is bureaucratic rationality's attempt to cleanse the empirical world of the annoying reality of contextuality. It's informed by the same logic that seeks to discover or generate '*best practices*' in teaching that can then be disseminated and imposed across multiple settings as a means of ensuring comparison and standardization. This neo-Fordist worldview regards contextuality as an annoying and unfortunate aberration, something to be removed so that the system of higher education can function smoothly. Trustees, governors and governments can be assured that predictable outcomes are assured and that the measures allowing league tables to rate institutional effectiveness are both reliable and valid.

The language of accountability and comparability assumes that higher education classrooms are a unitary phenomenon; that the same basic conditions for fostering student learning exist across classrooms and disciplines in multiple institutions. This assumption of comparability allows for the generation of standardized measures of learning and teaching. If the same basic process of teaching and learning happens in all higher education classrooms and with all students, then we can impose the same rubric to assess student learning and judge all teachers using the same basic evaluation instrument. This allows for institution C to be judged as better or worse than institution D or for teacher A's effectiveness to be rated next to teacher B's. Yet, as Stark and Freishtat's (2014) study of different *Student Evaluation of Teaching* (SET) forms observes, these forms typically 'don't measure teaching effectiveness. We measure what students say and pretend it's the same thing. We calculate statistics, report numbers and call it a day' (p. 9). There is the spurious scientism of percentages of students saying teacher did task A well or poorly. SET forms typically record students' judgments of how well teachers explained ideas, responded to questions, provided prompt feedback, encouraged discussion and so on. Such observations have no necessary connection to understanding the internal process of what or how any particular student learned.

The assumption of the unitary nature of teaching and learning is flawed. In fact, the opposite is the case. We should assume that in any single higher education classroom the way people learn, and the teaching approaches they find most helpful in developing new skills, processing new information and interpreting ideas are bewilderingly complex and idiosyncratic. The cultural, psychological, cognitive and political complexities of learning mean that teaching is never innocent; you can never be sure of the effect you are having on students or the meanings people take from your words and actions. Things are always more complicated than they at first appear.

So the overwhelming peculiarity of teaching and learning is that it is inherently unpredictable. To take the example of just one student learning one particular idea, say the process of photosynthesis. How this single student learns to understand correctly the nature of photosynthesis, and how she or he demonstrates that learning, involves a complex interaction of multiple variables. There is the matter of that person's particular brain chemistry that affects how the information about photo synthesis is processed. There is the level of readiness for learning he or she brings to the topic and the learning styles and habits she or he has developed over years. Does the student think verbally or visually? Is he or she used to group learning or to working independently?

Whatever is going on in the student's life will play a big part in determining how much attention he or she pays to learning the process of photosynthesis. A student experiencing emotional problems, trying to negotiate relationship difficulties, or exhausted from working two jobs to pay for college will experience a particular class on a particular day in a way that's very different from a student with none of these difficulties. The multiple realities that constitute just one student's life on one single day in one single class complicate enormously the simple-minded assumption that all students share a unitary reality and that therefore '*best practices*' for teaching these students can be generalized across multiple classrooms in multiple institutions.

And, of course, we've not even begun to discuss the contextuality of the teaching process yet. The particular ways that information about photosynthesis can be presented will work well with some students and not others. Students who think in a linear way and think textually will like being provided with a skeletal outline of lecture notes or a power point presentation dominated by lists of words. Students who think visually will want video and other images. Some students will respond well to analogy and metaphor, others will find this confusing. Some will be anxious to discuss their emerging understandings with peers, others will find this a waste of time. Providing space for students to ask clarifying questions will be appreciated by some whilst others will be annoyed by what they see as interruptions to the '*real*' work of teacher delivery.

Then we come to the teacher or teachers in the room. Each individual teacher brings a host of experiences, pedagogic preferences, assumptions about students and levels of familiarity with the topic being taught. There will be an implicit philosophy of teaching present with ideas about what good teaching looks like. Is it an expertly dazzling series of explanations and demonstrations or a discussion that's mostly student-led? Different teachers will welcome or become annoyed by frequent questions. For some it will the first time they've taught a unit, others will have decades of experience. Teachers may be distracted by a health problem, overwhelmed by a disintegrating personal relationship, intimidated by one or two students, disengaged because they know they won't get tenure, or resentful because they've been assigned to teach a unit they dislike or feel no familiarity with.

When you put these two sets of variables together – the multiple experiences, brain chemistries and learning preferences of the different students and those of the particular teacher – you have a snapshot of the inevitable contextuality of teaching and learning. There is no way in hell that the effects of a single teaching action such as starting off class by posing a question to the students can be predicted or measured. Depending on the make-up of students in class that day even the words making up a particular question itself will be heard in multiple and different ways. Then there are the different perceptions students have of the teacher. A racially mixed class will bring different assumptions about the teacher's credibility to the table. A female teacher working with an overwhelmingly male class may have her authority questioned in a way that wouldn't happen if the opposite were the case. The pervasive ideologies of White supremacy and patriarchy means that teachers who are women of colour will often be regarded as affirmative action hires. When I own up to making a mistake in class my positionality as an old White male means I'm rewarded for it; it's often approvingly described by students as my being '*vulnerable*'. But if a younger, female teacher of colour makes the same mistake her students may well start to doubt her credibility. The mistake is pounced on as an example of incompetence displayed by someone only hired because of her race or gender.

Finally, the contextuality of particular classrooms in particular departments is nestled within the wider contextuality of the political and cultural climate of the host institution and the broader society. In the countries in which I've worked there's been a normative privileging of speech and numeracy and linearity in both teaching methods and forms of assessment. Teachers talk as a means both of displaying authoritative command and inducting students into new bodies of knowledge. This happens in a linear fashion as students move incrementally from simple operations to more complex ones. The way students' increasing command of knowledge and ideas is assessed is through the language they use in classroom discussion and the kinds of questions they ask. I myself use the questions students pose in class as the best quick measure of how well the material is being understood.

But questions invariably privilege language. What about creative forms of assessment that allow students to present evidence of their learning in ways that fit the different ways people process information? To paraphrase Bohannon's (2011) provocative proposal, what about dancing your Ph.D.? Colleagues have often told me that I live in a postmodern world in which multiple subjectivities are the daily stuff of experience and in which identities are constantly reconfigured. If that's so then this world has yet to permeate the part of higher education I inhabit. Poems, graphics, videos, and music are accepted in the performance arts disciplines discussed by Emma Medland, Alison James and Niall Bailey in chapter 3 but I would imagine they would have a much harder time being accepted as a valid demonstration of the kinds of veterinary competence examined by Simon Lygo-Baker and Karen Young in chapter 2.

MUDDLING THROUGH AS THE HONORABLE RESPONSE TO PECULIARITY

In this final section I want to propose what seems to me to be the only response to the peculiarities of ideology and contextuality – muddling through. Our lives as teachers often boil down to our best attempts to muddle through the complex contexts and configurations that our classrooms represent. Studies of teachers' narratives (Preskill & Jacobvitz, 2000; Mattos, 2009) indicate how teachers muddle through their careers. They report their work to be highly emotional and bafflingly chaotic. Career counsellors and popular films may portray teachers as transformative heroes skilfully navigating classroom dilemmas to empower previously sceptical students, but actual teacher narratives (Harbon & Moloney, 2013; Shadlow, 2013) emphasize much more how teaching is riddled with irresolvable dilemmas and complex peculiarities. Of course administrators and politicians don't like to hear teachers say that they're muddling through, so this peculiarity is rarely spoken of publicly.

The notion of muddling through actually draws on the grand philosophical tradition of American pragmatism as represented by Dewey, Pierce, Emerson and James. Although pragmatism is now colloquially understood as opportunism, as doing anything to get what you want (as in a politician flip-flopping on electoral promises), its philosophical roots lie in the veneration of experience and experimentation as important guides to action. A classically pragmatic approach emphasizes the importance of continuous experimentation to bring about better (in pragmatist terms, more beautiful) social forms. For example, pragmatism argues that in building a democratic society we experiment, change, and tinker constantly to make democracy work better. Part and parcel of this effort is discovering our own, and others', fallibility. We make mistakes, adjust, broaden our experiences, seek out new perspectives, and talk to as many different people as possible. This is all done in the understanding that life is a constant process of experimentation as we pursue beautiful consequences.

Pragmatists hold that the way to become more knowledgeable about how to make democracy work better is through three strategies: (a) constant experimentation, (b) learning from mistakes, and (c) deliberately seeking out new information and possibilities. To me these are the three processes that are central to the process of muddling through teaching that I'm talking about. Muddling through is a kind of pragmatic dynamism requiring us to make constant adjustments based on emerging knowledge of how learning is experienced. Campuses are constantly adjusting to and incorporating new technologies, student bodies are becoming increasingly diverse, the information age and social media is changing how students communicate, and budgets are being cut even as numbers increase and contact hours lessen.

Teachers caught in these changes react pragmatically; they talk to as many colleagues as possible to borrow new ideas and exercises, they try things out in class that they hope will make more sense for a changing student body, and they try constantly to make sense of their experimentation. Team teaching is an inherently pragmatic pedagogy since it allows for mutual exploration of the different perspectives team members have on commonly shared classroom events. A good team is constantly debriefing the meaning of what happened in class and brainstorming what approaches might work best the next time the class meets.

Perhaps most importantly the best teachers respond to peculiarity by trying to find out how their students are experiencing their learning in multiple and complex ways.

They want to know which things are working well and which are misfiring so that they can make adjustments on the fly. In the last two decades an impressive body of work has emerged that provides examples of practices that teachers can use to gain this awareness. Evidence based teaching (Buskist & Groccia, 2011), classroom response systems (Bruff, 2009), and classroom assessment techniques (Dana & Yendol-Hoppey, 2009), all explore how to get inside students' heads. Once we have this information we are better placed to judge which of our assumptions are correct, what perspectives we've missed, and how to respond in the moment to what we're learning. This is part of what I regard as critically reflective teaching (Brookfield, 2017).

How do we muddle through the peculiarity of ideological control? If you're caught in a system that is essential irrational but that prides itself on being highly rational it's easy to experience a Kafkaesque alienation from your practice. To get tenure or stay in a job you have to teach material in prescribed chunks, at prescribed times and apply measures of assessment that have been externally imposed. If you are a junior lecturer who has little security or status it's a political risk to point out and critique the way these constraints inhibit rather than enhance learning. Yet to act as if there's no problem is to set yourself up for intra-psychic damage.

I think that dealing with the peculiarity of the ideologically framed nature of higher education requires a capacity to think and act politically. If you learn a measure of political shrewdness you can work in ways that are subversive to a dominant agenda. The first rule of political survival is to know what you are dealing with. As a newcomer to an institution who finds herself in an unfamiliar and possibly hostile situation, it is important to spend some time getting the lay of the land. I would suggest spending the first three to six months in a new job drawing a political map of the department, school or college. In departmental meetings, whole community e-mail conversations and senate gatherings try and work whose voice is taken seriously and where the power really resides. You need to work out what's really rewarded, what organizational symbols are revered, and how far the mission statement is taken seriously.

You also need to learn something of the cultural and political history of the institution. There is nothing worse than blundering in with a well meant, supposedly '*new*' suggestion only to find out later that a couple of years before you arrived the faculty spent six months considering, and then rejecting, something very similar. Probably the most important dimension of this anthropological work is researching the culturally approved language of the institution. A junior member of an organization who wishes to persuade those in power of the merits of a new and potentially threatening initiative would be well advised to couch their proposal in the language that is spoken and approved by those in power. In this regard knowing the mission statement is crucial. I have found that whenever I wish to propose something challenging, even threatening, the more I frame this using the language of the mission statement, the further I get.

Building alliances is also crucial to doing creative work that pushes back against the institutional culture. The one time I was fired I had no ally in the institution.

I had built no connections to other departments and I had never involved them in my programming. Consequently, no one had any stake in supporting me. When you can it's also good to rack up what Shor (1996) calls '*deviance credits*', organizational brownie points earned by publicly performing tasks crucial to institutional functioning. Examples might be serving on the alumni, library or diversity committee or helping to organize fund-raising events. Undertaking these tasks earns you a reputation as an organizational loyalist. They help you bank a large number of credits in the account of your organizational credibility. Winning awards from national or regional scholarly and professional bodies also helps your account grow.

If you have banked these credits, then you cannot be dismissed out of hand as a disloyal troublemaker when it comes time for you to take an oppositional stand. Your voice carries with it the institutional credibility of having performed these approved tasks. Cashing in your deviance credits at a strategic moment means you prize open a gap in which your concerns receive serious attention.

SUMMARY

In this chapter I have argued that a generally unacknowledged meta-peculiarity of higher education pedagogy is its emotional nature. I have then focused on two specific peculiarities; the fact that we work in a system under ideological control and the constant presence of contextuality. I believe that the best response to these peculiarities is to work in a way informed by American pragmatism; that is, to engage in the experimental pursuit of the beautiful consequence of improved student command of skills and knowledge.

REFERENCES

Bohannan, J. (2011, November). *Dance versus powerpoint: A modest proposal.* New York, NY: TED Talk. Retrieved July 2, 2013, from http://www.ted.com/talks/john_bohannon_dance_vs_powerpoint_a_modest_proposal.html

Brookfield, S. D. (2005). *The power of critical theory: Liberating adult learning and teaching.* San Francisco, CA: Jossey-Bass.

Brookfield, S. D. (2017). *Becoming a critically reflective teacher* (2nd. ed.). San Francisco, CA: Jossey-bass.

Browne, C. (2017). *Critical social theory.* Thousand Oaks, CA: Sage Publishing.

Bruff, D. (2009). *Teaching with classroom response systems: Creating active learning environments.* San Francico, CA: Jossey-Bass.

Buskist, W., & Groccia, J. E. (Eds.). (2011). *Evidence-based teaching.* San Francisco, CA: Jossey-Bass.

Chick, N. L., Haynie, A., & Gurung, R. A. R. (Eds.). (2012). *Exploring more signature pedagogies: Approaches to teaching disciplinary habits of mind.* Sterling, VA: Stylus Publishing.

Dana, N. F., & Yendol-Hoppey, D. (Eds.). (2009). *The reflective educator's guide to classroom research: Learning to teach and teaching to learn through practitioner inquiry.* Thousand Oaks, CA: Corwin Press.

Eisen, M., & Tisdell, E. J. (Eds.). (2000). *Team teaching and learning in adult education.* San Francisco, CA: Jossey-Bass.

Gurung, R. A. R., Chick, N. L., & Haynie, A. (Eds.). (2009). *Exploring signature pedagogies: Approaches to teaching disciplinary habits of mind.* Sterling, VA: Stylus Publishing.

Harbon, L., & Moloney, R. (2013). *Language teachers' narratives of practice*. Newcastle upon Tyne: Cambridge Scholars Publishing.
Horkheimer, M. (1974). *Eclipse of reason*. New York, NY: Continuum.
Horkheimer, M., & Adorno, T. W. (1972). *Dialect of enlightenment: Philosophical fragments*. Stanford, CA: Stanford University Press.
Marcuse, H. (1964). *One-dimensional man*. Boston, MA: Beacon Press.
Marcuse, H. (1969). *An essay on liberation*. Boston, MA: Beacon Press.
Marcuse, H. (1972). *Counterrevolution and revolt*. Boston, MA: Beacon Press.
Marcuse, H. (1978). *The aesthetic dimension: Toward a critique of Marxist aesthetics*. Boston, MA: Beacon Press.
Marx, K. (1961). *Economic and philosophical manuscripts* (T. B. Bottomore, Trans.). In E. Fromm (Ed.), *Marx's concept of man*. New York, NY: Frederick Ungar.
Mattos, A. M. A. (Ed.). (2009). *Narratives on teaching and teacher education*. New York, NY: Palgrave Macmillan.
Plank, K. M. (Ed.). (2011). *Team teaching: Across the disciplines, across the academy*. Sterling, VA: Stylus Publishing.
Preskill, S. L., & Jacobvitz, R. S. (2000). *Stories of teaching: A foundation for educational renewal*. Upper Saddle River, NJ: Prentice Hall.
Shadlow, L. K. (2013). *What our stories teach us: A guide to critical reflection for college faculty*. San Francisco, CA: Jossey-Bass.
Shor, I. (1996). *When teachers have power: Negotiating authority in a critical pedagogy*. Chicago, IL: University of Chicago Press.
Stark, P. B., & Freishtat, R. (2014, September 26). An evaluation of course evaluations. *Science Open*. Retrieved January 26, 2017, from https://www.stat.berkeley.edu/~stark/Preprints/evaluations14.pdf

Stephen D. Brookfield
College of Education, Leadership and Counseling
University of St. Thomas
Saint Paul, USA

KAREN M. YOUNG AND SIMON LYGO-BAKER

2. REDEFINING PROFESSIONALISM THROUGH AN EXAMINATION OF PERSONAL AND SOCIAL VALUES IN VETERINARY TEACHING

INTRODUCTION

This chapter was stimulated following a series of conversations between the two authors over a period of years working together on a range of learning and teaching projects. It is primarily based upon one particular planned conversation that sought to explore the journey Karen had made through her career to date and examined how the actions she had taken were influenced by the values with which she identifies. Simon, who acted as the '*interviewer*', is an academic developer who has worked with veterinarians in both the UK and the USA for a number of years. Karen is an experienced clinical pathologist who has been teaching in veterinary medicine since completing her training at the University of Pennsylvania. Both authors have significant interest in learning and teaching, including how these relate to definitions of professionalism, and have regularly explored what these notions may mean in the contexts within which they occur. Coming from different education systems (UK and USA), it is valuable to see how different interpretations have evolved and are understood.

In this conversation, the primary intention was to examine an individual perspective. Much of the previous literature has examined the process of socialisation into a professional role mostly from the perspective of the group (Levine & Moreland, 1994). Whilst acknowledging that every individual entering a role, in this case a teacher-clinician in veterinary medicine, is influenced by a set of group values, we believe that it is more complex and thus important to acknowledge and understand individual perspectives, including how these interact with and influence actions taken by those representing a particular professional role. We were therefore interested in the interplay that occurs between the individual and the group or groups encountered through time and how an identity is formed.

Whilst the literature examining how teachers within disciplines develop their identity has expanded (Danielewicz, 2001), it is limited within veterinary medicine (Dolby & Litster, 2015). Working with veterinary educators for the past fifteen years has given Simon insight into a series of tensions experienced by colleagues related to their identity, leading to discussions with colleagues at the Royal Veterinary College, the University of Wisconsin–Madison School of Veterinary Medicine, and the University of Surrey Veterinary School. Many of these conversations have involved Karen and often explored how professionalism and identity are linked and how individual experiences may shape our thinking about the education of past, current, and future students. Simon has previously undertaken research into how identities develop and how these are informed by values that are influenced by the personal experiences we have had and the social groups that we have encountered.

The basis for this framing came from the work of Breakwell (1986) and the notion that our actions are based on our values, which explain how we enact the role in which we are situated. According to Breakwell however, values are the consequence of a complex interplay between a set of personal values that are entirely unique to each individual and may stem from social values and factors such as critical incidents, experiences, and learning. Social values can be explained by the various groups that each person encounters, with the most obvious being those related to work. However, we begin to see the complexity when we explore the work environment, because within each work space different groups may exist, relating to particular roles that co-exist but have different functions. The social groups with which an individual interacts also exist beyond the work environment and may involve activities related to sport, faith, and community activities.

This conversation was based on exploring how these values and their influence on the identity an individual develops and recognises help us to explain professionalism through a less instrumental approach. Based on learning and teaching within the context of veterinary medicine, our approach was a semi-structured interview using a series of themes to explore how Karen's values had developed, had influenced her approach to learning and teaching, and were related to notions of professionalism. The themes, drawn out of previous informal conversations between the two and also other colleagues at a variety of events during a series of collaborations, included examining the role of the family at particular events or critical incidents and the impact of colleagues in shaping our approaches.

In previous conversations, both were interested in how notions of professionalism, especially related to how to teach professionalism, which requires colleagues to explore at the outset what they understand the term to mean, have emerged within broader discussions about curriculum. Experience has shown that there is no single definition with which everyone identifies. For some, professionalism relates to requirements defined by a particular professional body, whilst others feel it is more about interpretation and a nuanced approach based on context, which by definition continues to shift. Previous research by Simon suggested that these differences may occur because of the values that individuals draw upon (Lygo-Baker, 2006). It was therefore decided to explore Karen's journey to see if an anthropological approach might highlight important aspects to consider when trying to understand how professionalism can be interpreted.

As with any conversation, understanding the meaning expressed is potentially problematic, because meaning has likely evolved from past conversations and therefore is partly framed by assumed understanding from these past dialogues. Thus, such an approach may give rise to assumptions being made based on our tacit knowledge (Eraut, 2000), and, in addition, between colleagues there are elements where subjectivity may also occur (Diefenbach, 2009). However, the approach has the advantage that it is naturalistic (Lincoln & Guba, 1985). The two authors have regularly discussed the issues visited within the main conversation, and this provided an opportunity to frame those within a single event, to check understanding, and to examine perspectives that had previously surfaced, mirroring as closely as possible how the individuals would act in a typical conversation. It is acknowledged, however, that this conversation was different, as it had been arranged in advance and thus lacked some of the spontaneity of a typical conversation.

EARLY YEARS AND THE ROLE OF THE FAMILY

As formative experiences are often said to be significant in helping to understand how we progress as learners (Frome & Eccles, 1998), we started the conversation exploring what early memories Karen had and whether these shed any light on her journey to becoming a veterinarian and more particularly a clinical pathologist. We initially discussed early memories and whether Karen had always wanted to become a veterinarian. She noted that she had always *"loved animals"*, remembering how she would bring home stray cats and hide them in the family home. These animals, once discovered, would then be transported to the dairy farm of her grandparents to live out their lives. However, she does not remember at this stage having her heart set on any particular career.

It was clear from our discussion that her family was a significant factor in her early life. Taylor et al. (2004) argue that this is not surprising, as parents in particular tend to be significant people in the socialisation of their offspring. It might be expected then that Karen would move towards medicine given that her father was a physician and her mother had been a nurse. However, she spoke of how as a family they would discuss their days around the dinner table, and whilst her father displayed significant passion for his work, the discussions would take on a range of topics. As she and her siblings grew older the conversations increasingly turned to politics, and Karen became increasingly involved in a range of protests and activities. Her initial areas of academic study were seemingly far removed from veterinary medicine as she had an interest in liberal arts and languages, which led her to major in European history and Russian language. It may be that, whilst ultimately Karen migrated into a medical role, the initial familial socialisation surrounded the formation of values that encouraged behaviours around academic learning in broader subjects and an interest in varied interpretations.

MOVING INTO VETERINARY MEDICINE

Whilst at university Karen shifted towards science. She had continued to adopt stray cats and at some stage during her time at the University of Pennsylvania she remembered that she became interested in the possibility of pursuing veterinary medicine. As a consequence, she visited the veterinary medical school at the university and met with a number of the professors to see if she could become involved in any research projects. She became more familiar with the school and the people there and decided that this was something she wanted to pursue further. Initially this required an extra year of study after graduating to undertake additional required courses, such as organic chemistry. The extra work paid off, and although competition was fierce she was accepted into the program and stayed to do an internship, residency in medical oncology, and then a doctoral (PhD) program in hematopathology.

It was at this stage that Karen recognises that she first identified her interest in teaching. She remembered that she thought initially she had wanted to enter practice, but she also experienced a growing interest in academia. She noted that she liked both research and teaching, and as a consequence she decided that perhaps a role as an academic may be the appropriate route. Initially, however, the challenge was whether to focus on large (horses/cattle) or small (dogs/cats) animals, and she decided upon the latter. It was in part due to personal experience with a beloved cat, which died of leukaemia, that she then became interested in blood and bone marrow work; this led to a residency in medical oncology. Here again, individual experience was to play a significant part in the journey. Medical oncology was a relatively new field (Withrow et al., 2013) and Karen was the only resident. Unfortunately, her only mentor was seriously injured in a car accident, and Karen became responsible for much of the evolving service. This period was demanding, and she acknowledged "that it was very draining and so I wanted to take a step back". During her residency, she remembers participating in rotations in clinical pathology at the Hospital of the University of Pennsylvania (human, not veterinary, hospital), and this is where her path into pathology really began.

The shift to research and teaching occurred after meeting a faculty researcher with an MD degree, who studied bone marrow at the veterinary medical school. Karen met with him and decided to pursue graduate work, leading to the PhD degree. After completing the degree, she took a faculty position in clinical pathology at the University of Wisconsin–Madison, where she began to work with another clinical pathologist who had classical training in clinical pathology, which complemented and contrasted with her background and training in medical oncology. This proved to be a good partnership and perhaps highlighted the value of pluralism in the learning and teaching environment (Giselbrecht, 2009), something that Karen returned to at points in the conversation, acknowledging the challenge that it can present (Booth, 1986).

Much of the initial research examining the journey of individuals into '*professions*' began in the 1950s and 1960s (Atkinson & Delamont, 1985). Researchers claimed that it was during this journey that relevant competencies and values were acquired and became internalised by the new entrant. In many respects the individual and his or her identity became subsumed within the social values of the professional group, suggesting that in reality pluralism only occurs within a framework that recognises particular views and rejects others. Karen's journey, however, fits more clearly with those who have challenged this view, arguing instead that it is far less simple than individual values being completely overridden. Rather than a continuous and uniform experience, it is more likely to consist of conflicts of interest with people struggling to cope with the demands placed upon them, experiencing significant challenges to their own values and finding ways to deal with these. At certain points personal values will be compromised, although each person will potentially react differently to each particular dilemma (Lygo-Baker et al., 2008). Levine and Moreland (1994) suggest that, throughout this initial transition into the veterinary profession, Karen was exploring how her own values fit with those of the groups with which she was interacting. At times there were significant tensions, usually relating to different approaches of colleagues, requiring a re-examination of her values; then another period of evaluation would occur, testing and meeting new challenges and levels of reward between her own values and those encountered. Karen acknowledged that her initial experiences working in oncology brought tensions and challenged her approaches, testing the boundaries of pluralism, and that this has continued as she has worked with peers and learners throughout her career.

THE ROLE OF CURIOSITY, COLLABORATION, AND TEACHING

A further significant change occurred when Karen moved to take up a position at the University of Wisconsin – Madison. Here the shift to being fully immersed in a veterinary medical community was undertaken, working within a teaching hospital. According to Levine and Moreland (1994) Karen was now entering the second phase of socialisation, where an individual assimilates to a particular group, negotiating to maximise the contribution made. We discussed this period and what may have characterised these negotiations. Karen acknowledged that she had always been curious and her curiosity had been stimulated initially within family interactions, then at school and college. She remembered her teachers remarking she was always asking questions. She retains this today. Her own teaching approach is based on asking questions, leading to further questions, and she noted that she remains fascinated with new information and ideas extending across a range of subject areas. When she looked back she remembers how some of her own formative experiences at her own private school where she had some *"really excellent teachers"* encouraged this approach. She also remembered working at a summer camp, and, although at the time she viewed the role merely as a counsellor, she acknowledged that this experience may have had an impact on her interest in learning and working collaboratively with people, supporting their development.

It was winning a significant grant to study bone marrow that provided the next key learning point for Karen. She noted that it was at this point where she can clearly identify becoming less interested in aspects of competition. Instead she preferred collaboration, something she feels is an important element of who she is. Here Karen has continued to negotiate her role within her group. According to Levine and

Moreland (1994) this signifies the final stage of socialisation into a group, where the contribution the individual makes provides satisfaction and a feeling of commitment between the group and the individual stabilizes. It was during this period that she noted she "became more interested in education and applying my curiosity – and so shifted my focus to more education-related things".

Reflecting on this period Karen notes that she had also been missing the social element. The research and work she was undertaking was often isolated, and she notes that now she can see that what was of more interest was collaborating with others and sharing ideas. In many respects, this reflects back to those experiences she had with her family, discussing issues and sharing ideas and perspectives. It was this that Karen was perhaps beginning to seek again. According to McInnis (1993) there are potentially three sources of collective values we can interact with in higher education. These are the discipline, the department, and the institution. Karen recognises that as she became more comfortable at the university she started to branch out, becoming interested in knowing more about people and work across the campus beyond just the veterinary medical school. The influence of collective values, therefore, became greater. She noted, for example, that working on a funded project looking at peer review of teaching taught her a great deal about the possibilities of collaborative learning as she worked with people from theatre and business:

> This was a real eye-opener because this was a very collaborative approach. You could see differences and similarities, and I was attracted to these different approaches. I enjoyed coming back to the vet school and getting people together to talk about this so we could get people interested and not be isolated. I wanted to work on connections.

This notion of connections and drawing from other disciplines to develop new approaches that may challenge our own in constructive ways resonates within the work of Parker Palmer (2009). Palmer reflects that it is only through an examination of the self and the values that we hold that enables us to adapt to the different situations we face and to constantly question and therefore evolve as a teacher. He suggests that this reflects upon the integrity of the teacher, as she connects with others. Karen spoke at length about her interest in collaboration but also about recognising a need to resolve complex problems with others. In part she was drawn to clinical pathology because of the focus on problem solving, but also because it allowed her connect with "*almost all of the other services*". It was during this time that Karen recognised a shift in her primary identity from one she would describe as being a clinical pathologist. She stated that she saw her primary identity now as a teacher:

> I much more identify as being a teacher, as a person who wants to collaborate and cooperate with others so as to move the whole organisation forward. I think it is important to move the curriculum forward and not just within my own discipline but across disciplines, and that is one reason I work with colleagues

at other vet schools. I am not sure if I can fully describe this, but I feel as if I am someone who helps fit pieces together and bring ideas and people together. The goal, my goal, is to improve teaching and figure out how to optimise this.

Interestingly, in some respects this view challenges Piper's (1994) notion about academic development. For Piper, reflecting on the earlier work of Perkin, the teaching element is external to the primary identity. Piper argued that it is the subject that defines the professional and his or her identity. It is the subject that remains with the individual throughout his or her life, and the secondary element of being a teacher of the subject only exists whilst this is being enacted. Once the teaching duties cease, that transitory part of the identity ends, whereas the primary identity, in this case being a veterinarian, will remain. This was not fully recognisable to Karen, who in some ways reflected Rowland's (2002) assertion that the fragmentation that has occurred within professions has limited the identity to align with broad definitions. Rather than define ourselves broadly, Rowland argues that we seek comfort in great specialisation where our accountability and the subsequent challenge to our professionalism is less likely to cause us instability. Subsequently, while we may be a part of the veterinary profession, we are more likely to identify with a specialty within this. To some degree Karen recognised this, as she talked of clinical pathology with passion and pride, and this element of her identity is clearly an important aspect in framing who she is. However, this was not to exclude the broader notion of being a teacher within both clinical pathology, but also within veterinary medicine and even more broadly within clinical learning.

SHIFTING IDENTITY

As the conversation progressed, we talked about how Karen had shifted in her roles, considering where significant points or changes had occurred. Some of the '*critical incidents*' that had led to decisions were clearly more obvious than others. As part of this Karen considered the notion raised by Harre (1998) that we are all made of different selves that adapt to the situations and people we encounter. Karen was uncertain whether this was something she recognised and instead felt that, whilst she may shift her identity and certainly can see change over time, she recognised more the need to be adaptive and also to recognise that sometimes you have to accept that "you need to let the fish swim away from the boat because you are not going to influence them". She did note, however, that understanding who she was now required an appreciation of her whole history. Although she would once have felt that majoring in European history and Russian language did not have an impact on her current work, she now believes that it did. She argued that the liberal arts she experienced has significantly influenced how she now works.

When asked to explain this further, Karen considered how she believes that it is through dialogue and recognising difference that we can find alternative perspectives and subsequently enable progress. Her initial experience in liberal arts allowed her to have internal dialogues that influence her values today. This internal dialogue and those with her colleagues expose different personal epistemologies (Hofer & Pintrich, 2002) that help her form and reshape her values. There is therefore a balance within this of accepting other perspectives and learning from them and at the same time trying, as she said, to remain '*authentic*'. Previous research with veterinarians has shown that the values they hold influence what is perceived as effective performance and that this in part can be explained by different roles performed (Bolt et al., 2010). When this was raised, Karen said that some colleagues appear threatened by this approach, and she recognises barriers being erected through language and the fragmentation identified by Rowland (2002). Karen noted that she tries to find strategies to reduce this, but acknowledged that this was not always possible.

Considering this further Karen reflected that one of the challenges is that while there is great strength in pluralism, there are also challenges. Although the profession is encompassed under an umbrella term, there are a range of varied roles that exist, adding to the complexity and making agreed definitions problematic. A clinical pathologist undertakes a very different role than does an equine surgeon. Such fragmentation can provide a challenge to the provision of support, and each particular identity is important to those undertaking each particular role (Stryker, 1987). This identity, if it is explained at the level of specialised role (clinical pathologist) rather than the broader role (veterinarian), may undermine our attempts to define professionalism. For example, when a student enters the learning environment and anticipates learning to become a veterinarian, encountering this fragmentation or identity with a specialised role can cause difficulty in integrating elements of practice. Meyer and Land (2003) have suggested that this results in a curriculum that potentially focuses on a lot of fragmented knowledge and understanding that is harder to draw together and bring meaning to rather than on important threshold concepts that identify what it is to become a veterinarian and those transformative aspects that integrate knowledge and concepts. This may further undermine attempts to define professionalism.

Karen noted that fragmentation can be encouraged when people shroud their expertise in mystique, which she believes is unhelpful. In this sense professionalism becomes aligned with the notion of acceptance and entry into a group based on achievement of certain accepted requirements. Reflecting on this further, she said that there remain hierarchies; she remembered friends being surprised, for example, that she was not following her father into human medicine to become a '*real*' doctor. For Karen, this creates a problem with the notion of professionalism that for her has at its heart a sense of looking forward, to evolving our knowledge and understanding. So, rather than seeing professionalism as a way of creating barriers that only let in those who meet the criteria, it also has an element of inquiry, challenge, and discovery. For Karen the latter can often be encouraged by looking outside the known; this can be stimulated by others based on notions of pluralism.

When questioned further, Karen observed that her recognition of this came through time. Thinking back to teaching as a resident, she acknowledged that she felt she needed to know all of the information and to focus on ensuring she transmitted this to the students. She has a comfort now in helping people progress and achieve through provision of support, which may or may not include providing them with information. It is about helping people with their uncertainty, making expectations clearer, and having a dialogue that is joint and encourages development of potentially different voices and approaches that encourage pluralism. For Karen, this enables progress so that the profession can adapt and respond to the changes presented. Karen recognised that this comes in part from her growing expertise (Dreyfus, 2004). However, she noted that this was not a uniform journey from novice to expert, which resonated with research we had previously undertaken (Lygo-Baker et al., 2015). She reflected that, although experience can be a positive, with it also comes a growing gap between her and the learners. As a consequence, experience may at times get in the way, especially if it becomes based around routines (Hatano & Ingaki, 1986) that encourage set responses and actions. The key for Karen was to find ways to be adaptive and encourage other voices to enter the learning environment.

PROFESSIONALISM AND TEACHING

So what is professionalism and does it need to be redefined? Karen was keen to state that for her it is a "*set of authentic behaviours that promote learning*". For her these were respect, honesty, setting clear expectations, and remaining accountable. These were all dynamics working between the teacher and the students. In reality these can translate into what may appear to be mundane actions on the surface, such as arriving on time for class. However, they can also be complex dynamics where ethical and moral discussions occur around how to work with owners and arrive at agreed decisions. When we discussed these dynamics, there was a sense that they actually held the same properties as the definitions of threshold concepts (Meyer & Land, 2003). They tended to be behaviours that, once learned, were irreversible, acted as guides for careers, were integrative in that they pervaded all practice and behaviour of the individual, and were transformative in that they provided an identity linked to autonomy helping to define professional action. They were also troublesome. We discussed how these dynamics and authentic behaviours were actions that an individual executed, and, as such, they could be seen to be values, the determiners that influence the decisions we make (Inlow, 1972) and serve to guide us through different situations (Schwartz, 1994). Transcending different situations is what appears to provide a basis for seeing them as key aspects that lead to authenticity. Karen argued that for her authenticity is behaving in a way that is true to yourself and your values.

This turned our conversation to values and identity and whether this discourse could help us understand professionalism in ways that are not bounded by external factors alone and that recognise variation represented within any group. To remain authentic can be challenging, and Karen spoke of the challenge faced within teams when people have different values. She acknowledged that, whilst she will try and explore positions with people and seek alternatives and ways in which people can work without having to change or compromise alone, this is never easy and not always possible. She reflected on the complexity based on a variety of aspects such as seniority, length of service within an organisation, and support from peers.

As part of the programme when her own daughter had attended a wilderness camp, Karen spoke of being asked to consider her own values and what mattered most to her. After considerable thought, she said that the value that means most to her is kindness. For her, this relates directly to her understanding and interpretation of professionalism. In veterinary medicine you are dealing with life and death issues with owners and animals. In a teaching hospital you are also with students, residents, and interns who face significant competition; "to introduce kindness makes a real difference and you can end up navigating with this. It has to be kindness throughout, not sprinkled around." Karen reflected that kindness should not be confused with lower expectations. On the contrary, she argued that she is demanding. This took us to consider the value of success. Karen felt that this was also important. She noted that both these personal values were often challenged by others who do not share a similar outlook. For her, kindness and success should be feasible for everyone, and yet she noted that she is not convinced that colleagues always share this view, preferring instead to believe in hierarchy. For her, collaboration rather than competition is the key (although she did acknowledge that this did not apply when supporting her basketball and baseball teams!).

When asked what dangers her own values can present, Karen was very clear that within each value there are always areas that can be troublesome. She explained, for example, that as part of trying to be true to kindness there is a tendency that "you try and rescue people, and it is not always a good thing to rescue people, however natural it may appear; sometimes they need to learn to do things for themselves". Thinking back, Karen said she could remember times when her residents would come to her seeking a fix and she would take pleasure in providing solutions. Now, however, she has learned to be more selective, although she said she has to remain "*vigilant*" not to relapse too often. This reminded her of a talk about the "*invisible teacher*" she heard earlier in her career; initially this term made no sense to her, but as her career has developed she has embraced this concept as compatible with her values and embodying what she aspires to be as well as its link to professionalism.

REDEFINING PROFESSIONALISM

Research from the start of this century suggested that newly qualified veterinarians lacked key '*non-technical*' skills identified as necessary to meet the demands of the role even if they were technically competent (Lewis & Klausner, 2003). Lane and Bogue (2010) found that veterinary faculty were generally aware of the need to develop non-technical professional knowledge and skills in learners and that the majority of staff recognised that technical knowledge alone would not equip future veterinarians for their role in ways appropriate for contemporary practice. Thus, there is growing acknowledgement of the need to incorporate learning theory into the design and delivery of the veterinary curriculum in order to shift the emphasis away from technical knowledge alone (Schoenfeld-Tacher & Sims, 2013).

Despite this awareness, Dolby and Litster (2015) found that many faculty remain wedded to teaching techniques based primarily around the delivery of content knowledge. The curriculum remains heavily dependent on teaching that encourages a declarative approach from learners rather than demonstration of functioning knowledge. Such an approach may become more problematic when trying to teach non-technical skills, which are often the means through which technical knowledge and skills are displayed through application and associated processes, such as communication. Here we come to one of our major challenges and one that we have discussed over the years. How do we develop the non-technical skills of our learners, combining these with the technical skills and providing value for them? This challenge becomes apparent when we consider the learners we have all had the pleasure of working with. For example, when supporting teachers to pursue professional development there are many who can write an academically crafted narrative about the ways to teach; yet within the classroom they display no or very limited evidence of putting these teaching approaches into practice. So, whilst teachers can declare more effective approaches to teaching, they may not demonstrate them. The same occurs within veterinary medicine. Entering students are academically able and usually highly skilled at dealing with significant amounts of content knowledge in the short term. However, ask any of the staff to differentiate among graduating students who will be an effective veterinarian, and their impressions are unlikely to map neatly onto those who have the highest grades. Perhaps this is an inevitable outcome of competency-based learning and our focus on declarative knowledge, because such knowledge is easier to measure than application of knowledge and concepts.

The alternative is to provide a broader base to the curriculum, where professionalism does not equate to learning a great deal of information that may or may not be retained over time, as well as to develop some of the processes useful in applying this knowledge. We need to find a way of broadening our understanding of what constitutes the demonstration of professionalism as encompassing the *application* of declarative knowledge and the reasoning behind the judgments made. After all, it is becoming clearer that, while knowledge may be defined by teachers, the understanding of knowledge remains personal. Although a teacher may control delivery, the understanding of what the content means is constructed by an individual (Hay et al., 2008). Indeed, even though teaching teams believe they share a similar understanding of the material, this presumed consensus has also been shown to be flawed (Hay & Kinchin, 2006).

A tension that Karen recognised was that learners find themselves in an environment where there is a sense that people know how to make the '*right*' decisions. However, in truth these decisions sometimes lead to unsuccessful outcomes. The aim, however, is to ensure that when failure occurs it is not without thought, so

27

that procedures and actions result from an appropriate process. Professionalism is complex; there are elements of uncertainty and constant revision is required, something Karen noted. Although experience provides each individual with greater resources to assist with decision-making, not every situation encountered will be accompanied by a past experience that mirrors or is relevant to the current challenge with an obvious remedy. Past experiences may offer hints and opportunities; however, sometimes they obscure a particular path or action. Confidence is developed when acts have been experienced and repeated, leading to development of professional judgment and a greater ability to deal with uncertainty (Coles, 2003). This speaks to the '*craft*' of the discipline, perhaps reflecting Montgomery's (2006) claim that medicine is neither a science nor an art, but rather a practice.

Although redefining professionalism may appear extremely difficult, opportunities for change occur when the very notion of professionalism is contested and shaped by broader events. Within veterinary medicine, especially related to teaching, the term has surfaced increasingly. Discussions about the meaning of professionalism provide opportunities for faculty and students to consider how it can be understood and applied. Within some definitions there is a tendency to describe professionalism as a means to hold veterinarians accountable. Those who subscribe to this view likely believe that professionalism is defined by a professional body (the AVMA in the US or the RCVS in the UK) with increasing adherence to an audit culture based on regulation and rules. For some, this detracts from the opportunity for personal values to be a significant part of a veterinarian's role. Recent political events may promote a questioning of those in official positions within the professional organisation and a general lack of trust in those making decisions and may further reduce the autonomy of those in professional groups. For many there is a trade-off between autonomy and self-regulation, where the professionals hold the balance between bureaucracy and the market, which can seriously disrupt the public good. Durkheim (2013) defines this as a means through which professionals, in this case veterinarians, take responsibility for supporting the public good by giving away some autonomy in return for trust. Therefore, professionalism is about setting and maintaining high standards through which public trust then occurs. If the public believe that the social values of the group are increasingly subject to change and therefore can evolve, this may present an opportunity to recognise the pluralism that we have discussed in this conversation.

Rebalancing the personal values that shape an individual and the social values of the group may provide a more adaptable definition of professionalism, mirroring a more fluid world where change is constant (Beck, 1992). The veterinarian's role is acknowledged to be complex, requiring constant shifts in responding to different personalities (e.g., owners, animals, and peers). Allowing individual values to assume a more prominent role may offer greater connections with those in society, linking them to future veterinarians in ways that have not been possible when social values are unspoken and remain mysterious. There is a danger that group values constrain individuals and reduce the potential to act in particular ways (Stets & Burke, 2000); although this may curtail extreme actions, there was a possible response to this in our conversation: the notion of a moral base that emanates from the individual within the professional role (Nixon, 2001). Whilst there are responsibilities (drawn here from social values), there is a recognition that they are interpreted within a framework that is influenced by individual action. The challenge comes when an outlier exists, where actions push or go beyond the boundaries of how responsibilities have been defined or understood. At present, social or group values are emphasised and have the upper hand. Perhaps we should redefine the balance of power, where the individual has more authority to enact the role through the integration of personal and social values, adding a moral dimension to help regulate action. Without this, the profession is likely to continue to lose control of its autonomy as professionalism becomes defined by groups who increasingly exact influence from outside practitioners themselves, swayed further by public opinion.

This is not to argue that any professional group should remain independent of others. In this conversation, Karen identified her own passion and interest in looking outward rather than inward. Rather than looking towards those of a similar disciplinary persuasion, Karen spoke of examples where she has learned from others across the campus and beyond. These interactions were something that she valued immensely and believed had influenced her own development as both a veterinarian and an educator. The development of professionalism that is derived from personal values and how these interact with values of other social groups beyond a single discipline, in this case veterinary medicine, may be a way of beginning to address how we teach our future students. An example of just such an approach may come from work in medicine with Entrustable Professional Activities (EPAs) (ten Cate, 2013). EPAs are aspects of professional practice, defined as tasks or responsibilities to be entrusted to unsupervised execution by a trainee; a key aspect is that an EPA is independently executable. The basic principles of EPA-based education are simple: study the work undertaken by members of a particular professional group; identify the essential professional activities that all members must be able to do; provide learners with sufficient support and opportunities to master these activities; assess and sign-off learners in each activity as mastery is achieved. Once learners master all activities, they are ready to become a member of the professional group (Ross, 2015). They are the translation of competency into practice, a key aspect of the transition from learner to practitioner. Here the emphasis shifts to the *process* and can be based on the personal values that an individual brings with her or him, rather than merely trying to conform to those displayed by experienced teachers.

REFERENCES

Atkinson, P., & Delamont, S. (1985). Socialisation into teaching: The research which lost its way. *British Journal of Sociological Education, 6*(3), 307–322.

Beck, U. (1992). *The risk society: Towards a new Modernity.* London: Sage Publications.

Bolt, D., Witte, T., & Lygo-Baker, S. (2010). The complex role of veterinary clinical teachers: How is their role perceived and what is expected of them? *Journal of Veterinary Medical Education, 37*(4), 387–393.

Booth, W. (1986). Pluralism in the classroom. *Critical Inquiry, 12*(3), 468–479.
Breakwell, G. (1986). *Coping with threatened identities*. London: Psychology Press.
Coles, C. (2003). Learning about uncertainty in professional practice. In L. S. Sommers & J. Launer (Eds.), *Clinical uncertainty in primary care* (pp. 47–72). New York, NY: Springer.
Danielewicz, J. (2001). *Teaching selves: Identity, pedagogy, and teacher education*. Albany, NY: State University of New York Press.
Diefenbach, T. (2009). Are case studies more than sophisticated storytelling?: Methodological problems of qualitative empirical research mainly based on semi-structured interviews. *Quality and Quantity, 43*(6), 875–894.
Dolby, N., & Litster, A. (2015). Understanding veterinarians as educators: An exploratory study. *Teaching in Higher Education, 20*(3), 272–284.
Dreyfus, S. (2004). The five-stage model of adult skill acquisition. *Bulletin of Science Technology & Society, 24*, 177–181.
Durkheim, E. (2013). *Professional ethics and civic morals* (2nd ed.) (Routledge Classics in Sociology). Hoboken, NJ: Taylor & Francis.
Eraut, M. (2000). Non-formal learning and tacit knowledge in professional work. *British Journal of Educational Psychology, 70*(1), 113–136.
Frome, P., & Eccles, J. (1998). Parents' influence on children's achievement-related perceptions. *Journal of Personality and Social Psychology, 74*(2), 435–452.
Giselbrecht, M. (2009). Pluralistic approaches: A long overdue paradigm shift in education. *Scottish Languages Review, 20*, 11–20.
Harre, R. (1998). *The singular self: An introduction to the psychology of personhood*. London: Sage Publications.
Hatano, G., & Inagaki, K. (1986). Two courses of expertise. In H. Stevenson, J. Azuma, & K. Hakuta (Eds.), *Child development and education in Japan* (pp. 262–272). New York, NY: W. H. Freeman & Co.
Hay, D. B., & Kinchin, I. M. (2006). Using concept maps to reveal conceptual typologies. *Education and Training, 48*(2–3), 127–142.
Hay, D. B., Wells, H., & Kinchin, I. M. (2008). Quantitative and qualitative measures of student learning at university level. *Higher Education, 56*(2), 221–239.
Hofer, B., & Pintrich, P. (Eds.). (2002). *Personal epistemology: The psychology of beliefs about knowledge and knowing*. Mahwah, NJ: Lawrence Erlbaum Associates.
Inlow, G. (1972). *Values in transition*. Hoboken, NJ: John Wiley & Sons.
Lane, I. F., & Bogue, E. G. (2010). Perceptions of veterinary faculty members regarding their responsibility and preparation to teach non-technical competencies. *Journal of Veterinary Medical Education, 37*(3), 238–247.
Levine, J. M., & Moreland, R. L. (1994). Group socialization: Theory and research. *European Review of Social Psychology, 5*(1), 305–336.
Lewis, R., & Klausner, J. (2003). Nontechnical competencies underlying career success as a veterinarian. *Journal of the American Veterinary Medical Association, 222*(12), 1690–1696.
Lincoln, Y., & Guba, E. (1985). *Naturalistic inquiry*. London: Sage Publications.
Lygo-Baker, S. (2006). Re-evaluating values: The impact of academic developers. *International Journal of Learning, 12*(4), 11–18.
Lygo-Baker, S., Kingston, E., & Hay, D. (2008). Uncovering the diversity of teachers' understanding of their role: The importance of individual values. *International Journal of Learning, 15*(5), 245–253.
Lygo-Baker, S., Kokotailo, P., & Young, K. (2015). Developing confidence in uncertainty: Conflicting roles of trainees as they become educators in veterinary and human medicine. *Journal of Veterinary Medical Education, 42*(4), 364–372.
McInnis, C. (1993). *Academic values under pressure*. Melbourne: CSHE.
Meyer, J. H. F., & Land, R. (2003). Threshold concepts and troublesome knowledge 1: Linkages to ways of thinking and practising. In C. Rust (Ed.), *Improving student learning: Ten years on* (pp. 412–424). Oxford: OCSLD.
Montgomery, K. (2006). *How doctors think: Clinical judgment and the practice of medicine*. Oxford: Oxford University Press.

Nixon, J. (2001). Not without dust and heat: The moral bases of the new academic professionalism. *British Journal of Educational Studies, 49*(2), 173–186.

Palmer, P. (2009). *The courage to teach.* Hoboken, NJ: John Wiley & Sons.

Piper, D. W. (1994). *Are professor professional?* London: Jessica Kingsley.

Ross, M. (2015). Entrustable professional activities. *The Clinical Teacher, 12*(4), 223–225.

Rowland, S. (2002). Overcoming fragmentation in professional life. *Higher Education Quarterly, 56* (1), 52–64.

Schoenfeld-Tacher, R., & Sims, M. H. (2013). Course goals, competencies, and instructional objectives. *Journal of Veterinary Medicine Education, 40*(2), 139–144.

Schwartz, S. (1994). Are there universal aspects in the structure and content of human values? *Journal of Social Issues, 50*(4), 19–45.

Stets, J. E., & Burke, P. J. (2000). Identity theory and social identity theory. *Social Psychology Quarterly, 63*(3), 224–237.

Stryker, S. (1987). Identity theory: Developments and extensions. In K. Yardley & T. Honess (Eds.), *Self and identity: Psychosocial perspectives* (pp. 89–103). Oxford: John Wiley & Sons.

Taylor, L. C., Clayton, J. D., & Rowley, S. J. (2004). Academic socialization: Understanding parental influences on children's school-related development in the early years. *Review of General Psychology, 8*(3), 163–178.

ten Cate, O. (2013). Nuts and bolts of entrustable professional activities. *Journal of Graduate Medical Education, 5*(1), 157–158.

Withrow, S. J., Page, R., & Vale, D. M. (2013). *Withrow and MacEwen's small animal clinical oncology* (5th ed.). St Louis, MO: Elsevier Saunders.

Karen Young
School of Veterinary Medicine
University of Wisconsin
Wisconsin, USA

Simon Lygo-Baker
Department of Higher Education
University of Surrey
Guildford, UK

EMMA MEDLAND, ALISON JAMES AND NIALL BAILEY

3. "MESSY AND PRECISE"

Peculiarities and Parallels between the Performing Arts and Higher Education

INTRODUCTION

This chapter is based on a set of organic and emergent conversations between an Academic Developer at the University of Surrey (first author), Director of Academic Quality and Development at the University of Winchester (second author) and a Senior Musical Director and Teaching Fellow from the Guildford School of Acting (third author). Through a series of discussions based on personal reflections, conversations with a range of performing arts colleagues (including practitioners, educators, managers and researchers), and a consideration of the literature, the three authors reflected upon the pedagogical challenges that are '*peculiar*' to the performing arts across both university and conservatoire provision. The performing arts was chosen as the focus of this chapter in view of three things: the relative dearth of pre-existing literature on performing arts pedagogy; the perception that the performing arts do not always sit neatly within the formal and standardised practice of higher education, and; the perception of the pedagogical creativity and experimentation often associated with them.

Experience within the performing arts industry is often a prerequisite for staff, and the teaching cultures are as diverse as the disciplines that are subsumed within it. Discussion focused largely on both the peculiarities and parallels emerging when personal, disciplinary and institutional identity, values and aspirations intersect. Views emerging from such discussion highlighted this intersection while also expressing a range of strong positive and negative feelings as to how the performing arts fare within the present-day frameworks of higher education processes and regulations. The concept of "*messy precision*", therefore, captures the conflict emerging when attempting to map the approaches, content and methods associated with the performing arts (that may appear "*messy*" to the outsider), against both industry expectations and the standardised processes and criteria set by the higher education institution. The concept is particularly apparent in relation to the assessment of performing arts students' work that is necessarily subjective and interdisciplinary in nature.

As a means of providing structure to the chapter, the discussion will be divided into two themes: (1) Disciplinary versus Personal and Institutional Identity, and; (2) Personal versus Disciplinary and Institutional Values. Each theme will consider the peculiarities and parallels emerging when personal, disciplinary and institutional values, identities and aspirations intersect. The order of themes is not based on a hierarchy of importance nor is it an exhaustive list, but rather a reflection of our own organic dialogue and emergent realisations. As such, these themes are interlinked and their focus necessarily overlaps.

DISCIPLINARY VERSUS PERSONAL AND INSTITUTIONAL IDENTITY

Before embarking on a consideration of the result of the intersection of disciplinary, personal and institutional identity within the performing arts, the concept of identity must first be outlined.

Within the scope of this chapter, the authors' understanding of identity aligns most closely with Glynis Breakwell's (1986) theorisation of the concept. Within her book, Breakwell (ibid) highlights identity as being a highly complex and dynamic concept which definition is largely dictated by the methodological and philosophical foundations of the particular theory adopted. At their most expansive, attempts at defining the concept of identity tend to combine personality, character and self-concept whilst emphasising the influential nature of experience and the ever changing social context. A further distinction raised by Breakwell (1986) that is relevant to this chapter, relates to the importance of distinguishing between social identity and personal identity. This she achieves through the grounding of social identity within social position, group memberships, status and interpersonal relationships, describing personal identity as 'free of role or relationship determinants' (p. 14). As a result, this section considers the intersection between social identity (i.e. disciplinary and institutional identity) and personal identity. Although it should be acknowledged that it would be a difficult task to define personal identity other than in relation to social context and history, which serves to identify the potential for both parallels and conflict between the two.

Interestingly and, perhaps most pertinent to this chapter, Breakwell (1986, p. 16) notes that:

> …it is at times when they [personal and social identity] clash that people are most acutely aware that they have both a public and private self…people tend to exhibit a habitual predisposition to focus on one aspect or the other in coming to a solution. People have habits with regard to which aspect of the self they will allow to dominate. A focus on the private self is correlated with a concern for '*personal*' aspects of identity (emotions, feelings, thoughts, goals, aspirations), whilst emphasis on the public self is closely associated with attaching importance to social aspects of identity (group memberships, social influence, social interaction patterns).

In other words, behavioural reaction is shaped by the aspect of self that is perceived to be most important, thus serving to reveal ones '*real self*' through the surfacing of personal values that underpin personal identity.

One of the key aspects of the social context that Breakwell (1986) identifies as influential to identity is, at the time of writing, the vote in the UK for the British Exit from the European Union (EU), dubbed '*Brexit*', which has contributed to pessimism about the future of the arts and cultural education. In the publication entitled '*The Stage*' (Hemley, 2016), former National Theatre Director Nicholas Hytner, has questioned why borders might be imposed on the free exchange of talent and roles in a post-Brexit world. This wider erecting of boundaries summons some of the more localised territory markings that we discuss in this paper. The negative impact of leaving the EU has also been conjured by Equity and the Musicians Union (ibid), while the Creative Industries Federation, reported in the new Statesman (Collier, 2016), highlights the need to safeguard the future of the UK's arts, creative industries and cultural education.

Against this theoretical and social backdrop, this section focuses on the relationship of the performing arts to the wider world of art and design, and on the relationship between the disciplines that are subsumed within the performing arts domain. It considers how different modes of delivery are grounded within social and personal identity, and it considers the relationship between professionalization and academic freedom.

The Nature of the Performing Arts

The category '*performing arts*' is too broad to make instantly explicit the variations within it; it suggests the generic while housing the distinctive. Courses focus variously on the material contribution to theatre, others on production, others on the performers above all else, and others still are most interested in the exploration, reinvigoration and embodiment of text. Beliefs about the nature of the performing arts run along a continuum. At one end is the conviction that they are distinct in character from all other kinds of arts and design, and at the other that they cross all kinds of boundaries and are inherently interdisciplinary. In the words of one course leader:

> …they are the glue that links performance to subjects such as fashion, architecture, spatial and interior design, and object-based courses.

The very notion that there are two polar positions as to the nature of performing arts is, therefore, one that needs to be qualified and one that highlights a tension relating to the social identity of those operating within the domain of the performing arts.

Within the disciplines that are subsumed within the domain of the performing arts (e.g. Acting, Dance, Musical Theatre etc.) there are important matters of territories (Becher & Trowler, 2001), histories and hierarchies at play. The origins of different performing arts courses and schools, and competing tendencies between certain areas and models, affect how new developments are perceived today. In one institution with a longstanding involvement in scenography there has been a distinct espousal of a practice and philosophy wherein theatre designers are not simply working in the service of the playwright or director but have a creative contribution to make in their own right, perhaps equal to actors and directors. Such equality is not always evident; some design or generalist performance courses criticize acting courses as being there to create "*pretty*" performances and show off the actors. However one theatre designer argued that it was theatre design that revolutionized the West End, while also lamenting the disparities in earning power – makers often earning more than the designer did.

Further tensions emerge between drama (often described as "*more academic in nature*") and acting and performance (requiring a different set of skills that are not as aligned with the traditionally academic skills), where the cultures or 'taken-for-granted values, attitudes and ways of behaving' (Becher & Trowler, 2001, p. 23) do not align, and result in tensions between both espoused and enacted practice. In other words, whilst a department might be guided by an underlying philosophy of collaboration, a clash in cultures between its disciplines might result in failure to enact the espoused, and the creation of tensions that can make a truly interdisciplinary approach (Spelt et al., 2009) almost impossible. For example, tensions have arisen between a design and production department led by a Head of Department who wished to take the course in a completely different direction. This new direction involved a change of focus to that of digital design. However the performance department's required outputs are production utilising a more traditional approach in order to match against industry expectations, which dictated against this new direction. From one perspective, it might seem that the performance department is stifling the creativity and development of the Head of the Department. But from another perspective, perhaps the real issue is that attention is being focused on developing content and modes of delivery to match standardised learning outcomes as a means of achieving a constructively aligned curriculum (Biggs, 1999) that the institution is required to provide, rather than with the student and their ongoing training or learning journey within the discipline. This clash between the social (i.e. institutional requirements) and personal identities of the practitioners involved can result in tensions that force individuals to reveal their real selves through which aspect of their identity they allow to dominate. For instance, one colleague noted: "the students are not an interruption to the process. They are the process". Thus highlighting the dominance of personal identity over the institutional social identity, which was perhaps the focus of the Head of Department mentioned above.

Performing Arts Education – Content and Modes of Delivery

Misconceptions and tensions (perceived and otherwise) relating to social identity can occur within and between performing arts housed in different structures. Whilst university-based programmes must align to institutional regulations and prescribed modes of delivery that focus more on the academic side of the performing arts, a conservatoire-based programme has a greater focus on practice-based performance. The barriers and disconnects that emerge between the differing philosophies and identities underpinning these quite diverse modes of delivery are considered, and the benefits and challenges associated with collaborative practice are discussed.

Where a performance-based organisation is integrated into pre-existing institutional structures, adherence to the 15 credit module approach[1] can create tensions between the personal and social identity of educators. For instance, in the early stages of performance training, the individual skills and techniques of spoken voice, singing voice, acting techniques, dance, movement, physical acting etc., are the main focus, but under the 4×15 credit modules per semester structure they are shoehorned into sometimes clumsy combinations. Furthermore, the idiosyncratic rules of assessment weighting percentages, allowable timings of assessment etc., can skew the picture. In later years of training, a students' performance in the daily or weekly dance, singing, voice classes, should come second in importance to their performance in public/industry facing activities, though engagement in classes is vital for students to maintain industry standard skills in these areas. However, to be able to justify the staff resources (hours therefore money) dedicated to this support activity, they too find themselves skewed out of proportion and torn between the competing pressures of personal versus social identity aspects.

Snobberies and tensions were felt to exist between variants of the disciplines: for one person it was essential to "*protect the nature of the conservatoire*" while for another dedicated drama schools were perceived to have been "*spoiled rotten*" in terms of time and resource allocation, the ability to retain small classes, and operate outside the constraints of a larger institution (in the past). These were perceived to exist between kinds of performance housed within different structures; the drama department within a traditional university (text-based, "*properly academic*"), the drama school within an art school, the art school within the university, the conservatoire model alongside the generalist performance-for-all qualifications. Some of the barriers between them tend to be in terms of identity, not least where a drama school has been imported into a bigger organisation and perceives challenges to its identity, or where jealousies erupt over the number of hours the school can allocate to its courses. There are also misconceptions: where an institution is promoting a culture of opting in and out of different units, it is not always appreciated that a pick n' mix approach, say, to "*doing a bit of ballet*" cannot work within a conservatoire model, where developing and stretching the body for dance is a matter of long term preparation and consideration for physical wellbeing are paramount.

The collision between dip-in and dedicated models of delivery is often due to a matter of competing educational aspirations and structures – in one, variety and collaboration are to the fore, while in the other focus and single-minded investment are respected principles. For one respondent collaborations happened "*organically*" – with a project growing out of an emotionally invested and aesthetically pleasing "*object*" (e.g. the performance) which the writer and director then build narratives around. There is a symbiotic relationship between all the players, none of whom have a purpose for existence without the other. However, while the respondent and other educators attest that the performing arts are by definition collaborative, such collaborations between different models of provision are not always straightforward in view of the potential for a clash of cultures (Becher & Trowler, 2001). Collaborative projects may be the norm but are often dreaded as they can fall apart through participants not fulfilling their roles and responsibilities adequately. The ability to share units across the performing arts, as we have already seen, can be problematic. A move towards interdisciplinary collaborations is often resisted because each side of the equation have different views of what the other can contribute: students on a generalist performance course may be willing and enthusiastic to work with their drama school colleagues on a production, but are perceived by the latter to have neither the talent nor the professionalism to be up to the task.

While this may sound harsh, it is an illustration of the disconnects that can exist between the identity, aspirations and values of institutions, disciplines and individuals (including the profession and industry) and the competing cultures that surround each of these. Here we see a clash both between social identity (i.e. institutional and disciplinary) and personal identity, but also between the social identities of different groups (i.e. those involved in the provision of dip-in versus dedicated models of delivery) and aspects of personal identity that are interlinked with these differences in provision.

It should be noted, that we are not suggesting that in every situation where performance forms part of a multidisciplinary offer that these automatically exist. However, our conversations with colleagues working in diverse organisational contexts indicate that sensitivity and flexibility are valuable facilitators in supporting cohabitation between different partners. The cultures of a '*traditional*' UK art school, a conservatoire, a drama school and a university can be distinct and great strides are needed to see how they may integrate at least in some measure. These might manifest in the desire by a performance course to explore experimental practice while its acting counterpart may demand external input to ensure high quality production values and be suspicious of an amateur, in-house offer. The need for organisational and time management skills for the stage team may be at odds with some of the freer, exploratory practices of fine art students. The resource-heavy, out-of-hours culture of a drama course may sit unevenly with other kinds of design provision. Students on a drama course may be excellent at theoretical analysis and textual interpretation, while those on design courses will have a visual articulacy that the former lack. It is not given that each will possess both.

The Professionalization of Performing Arts Teachers

This sub-section focuses on how respondents viewed the professionalization of performing arts teaching; whether they welcomed it as necessary, or saw it as an assault on creative and autonomous freedoms. Professionalization has been posited as an encroachment on practitioner (i.e. personal) or disciplinary (i.e. social) identity; however in discussion it generated diverse views.

Despite the areas of conflict outlined above, many performance teams remain extraordinarily resilient and optimistic in the face of their challenges. This is driven by passion for the subject and belief in its value, and shaped by a resourceful approach to finding ways of working within the system. In other words, this is driven by a commitment to one's personal identity. The move to professionalise teaching within the arts was seen by certain respondents as a natural formalisation of what they were doing already. However, they noted that if they are working professionally outside the university for most of the week, this inevitably impacts on the kind of involvement they are able to dedicate to teaching and learning on courses. This offers a clear example of how the intersection between the personal and social identities are influenced by experience and the social context (Breakwell, 1986). Furthermore, one participant felt that while there is a perception that everyone should be a qualified teacher, not everyone wants to be. Their identity is bound up in practice, not in education. In other words, the multiple aspects of social identity can force one to view the dual roles, that of practitioner and educator, as distinct and therefore in competition rather than complementary in nature. This, in turn, can lead to the perception that one must choose between ones professional versus pedagogical role, rather than viewing them as two sides of the same mutually beneficial coin. This is no more apparent than where more value is placed on academic elements of a performance degree than the "*practical doing elements*". One practitioner explained that "if the learning experience is fully active and all-absorbing then you don't need teacher training" compared to other, more "*boring*" modes of delivery with lectures and PowerPoints.

Where dissatisfaction with the context exists, this can lead individuals to attempt to alter the values and beliefs of a group and where alterations to the social context entail an individual to behave in new ways; this can lead to quick and more wide-ranging modifications to identity. However, 'changes in identity are not inevitable but resistance is more difficult and more traumatic' (p. 41). Breakwell (1986) explains that 'identity [comprising attitudes, beliefs and emotions] directs action… identity and action are dialectically related' (p. 43), therefore, one can only gain insight into another individual's identity via his/her actions. However, as Clegg (2008) points out, 'Much of the day-to-day talk and grumbling…works to establish common bonds, as a way of dealing with difficulties, and in part represents small acts of defiance and resistance' (p. 342) and thus the creation of a community or shared social identity.

PERSONAL VERSUS DISCIPLINARY AND INSTITUTIONAL VALUES

As with the previous section, before embarking on a consideration of the result of the intersection of personal, disciplinary and institutional values within the performing arts, the concept of values must first be considered.

Higher education is a '*value-laden enterprise*' (Harland & Pickering, 2011, p. 1). However, as Macfarlane (2004) acknowledges, discussions of values relating to teaching in the higher education arena have largely disappeared and received comparatively little consideration within the literature surrounding professionalism in higher education. One exception takes the form of Nixon (2001b), who highlights the importance of the interplay of values at not only the individual and group practice level, but also at the organisational structures level. Indeed Harland and Pickering (2011) echo this sentiment by emphasising the influence of the value context within which all teaching takes place in higher education. They note that '…values influence the way we see the world and how we operate in it, and in this sense, nothing is "value free"' (p. 3). Their theorisation of values in higher education also highlights the interplay between the contemporary values of the institution, our past experiences and personal and professional identities, pointing out that:

> …values are necessarily the driving force behind all our thinking and that they are lived out day to day in our practices, making them prominent in academic life presents us with great difficulties. Values are difficult to express, often hidden in our thoughts and are liable to be overlooked while we get on with the daily business of research and teaching. (Harland & Pickering, 2011, p. 1)

Any discussion of values, therefore, has clear linkages with the discussion of personal and social identity in the above section.

With the increase in tuition fees, reduction in resources, and rise in the prominence of the student experience and league tables, which Nixon (2001a) describes as the marketization of university education, the pressure of performativity is ever increasing. Indeed, Nixon (2001b) describes the academics working within this increasingly stratified and managerialist higher education system as becoming 'increasingly isolated, while also becoming increasingly accountable' (p. 73). What the increasing accountability seen in higher education institutions seemingly fails to acknowledge, however, is the potential conflict between the individual, group practice level and organisational structures levels and that, 'when push comes to shove, practitioners must, in the interests of their own professionalism, back the values implicit in practice' (Nixon, 2001b, p. 77). This can lead to a number of areas of contestation in contexts where a significant number of educators have strong and active professional identities, such as the performing arts. In other words, this tension between the vocation as educator and the often primary disciplinary or professional identity (i.e. different aspects of social identity as has been highlighted in some of the above examples from practice), it is often the latter that provides the 'main external point of reference… they will subscribe to this group's norms and values' (Macfarlane, 2004, p. 1).

In view of this theoretical and social background, this section focuses on the perceived devaluation of the performing arts and its impact on the values (and identity) of staff, which considers programmes both within and outside institutional structures. From within institutional structures, the potential impact of assessing the performing arts on both students and teachers, particularly with regard to how the continuous nature of performance sits within institutional processes and regulations is then considered.

The Nature of the Performing Arts

Recent political pronouncements and educational initiatives have relegated the creative arts, design and media to a secondary position compared to STEM subjects and industries. An obvious example is the proposed English Baccalaureate (EBacc) qualification which demotes arts (including drama) and music to activity outside the core curriculum. It is clear, however, that threats are perceived not simply from outside the performing arts, but from within them also. Some interviewees touched on comparison between a conservatoire model of performance and higher education provision, which is deemed to be less rigorous. Similarly they identify the tensions that can erupt when a performing arts organisation is subsumed into a pre-existing higher education institution. Here, Nixon's (2001b) call to 'back the values implicit in practice' becomes muddied in view of the preponderance of staff who must embrace the dual role of active professional practitioner and academic educator and who, when push comes to shove, may identify most closely with the professional practitioner role that serves to characterise their social identity.

The reduction of government funding, accommodation of different funding models and the imposition of often ill-fitting institutional regulations have had a major influence on contemporary performing arts education, including restrictions of resources and the scaling down of contact hours. Indeed, a number of practitioners went as far as arguing that performing arts education is being '*systematically attacked*' through these reductions in funding, and that recent educational policy decisions have resulted in the demotion of the arts and design disciplines. One respondent noted that:

> ...there is a robust business case to be made for performing arts and theatre design: in company with other creative disciplines they make a significant contribution to national GDP while their students contribute to culture in real and material ways.

The advent of neo-liberalist values, which imply that a market-driven learning economy is more valuable than one with sociocultural or humanitarian significance, provokes both anger and resignation; the shrinking of funding for arts education has further given rise to the adoption of workload models and drives to prove productivity and efficient use of time. Use of these is seen as systematically extinguishing goodwill among staff who may have given over and above in terms of their time and expertise in the past, but who now, forced to account for every second of their employment hours to prove value for money, are considering withdrawing it. This is resulting in deepening tensions between institutions and their staff due, in part, to the contestation that it introduces between an individual's personal and social identity and the inclination towards backing the values that underpin the identity of the '*real self*' (Breakwell, 1986).

There are also knock-on effects elsewhere, for example, one university with theatre spaces was prioritising commercial rental of these, rather than safeguarding them for in-house use, as the need to generate income means courses cannot afford to hire them themselves. Here we see the tensions emerging between the marketization of higher education and the values that underpin both personal and social identity. Other financial constraints impact on the design and delivery of performing arts courses and can generate tensions within the institution. As all Drama schools have to be accredited by DramaUK there are certain expectations that what is delivered will match the DramaUK full cost model. This means that cross-subsidising has to occur to ensure the right number of hours are offered each week; as every drama school has to find a funding model to support the hours, and may receive no subsidy from the university, other means have to be found to generate the income required (e.g. through charging for auditions and sources of additional income). Where the personal, group practice and organisational structures level values do not align, the urge to revert back to what is viewed as the central point of reference (i.e. the values underpinning one's professional identity) is strong and can lead to a stalemate.

There are clear disparities between a conservatoire model of performance with a focus on dance, acting and music, which offers high-level vocational training with specific staff-to-student ratios, space requirements and minimum levels of resource, and an institution-based performance course. The former may offer 35 hours a week contact time while in certain university departments 10 is the average. In turn, time constraints within an institution may translate into negative perceptions of time – that there is too much teaching going on from a management point of view, to the concern that there is too little from the course team's position. This area of contestation is no more apparent than during the integration of a performance-based organisation into pre-existing institutional structures. Here, disparities are exaggerated and tensions heightened due, in large part, to a clash between the values of the institution versus those of the individual staff. Comments such as "That's not the way we do it round here" encapsulates the competing values surrounding the purpose of higher education, which is met with varying degrees of compromise. As Breakwell (1986) points out, where alterations to the social context entail an individual to behave in new ways, this can lead to quick and more wide-ranging modifications to identity, although 'changes in identity are not inevitable but resistance is more difficult and more traumatic' (p. 41).

Where compromise is not achieved, there is a perception amongst staff that their personal values (and identities) have been diluted and that the performance-based organisation "*family*" has been largely replaced by the "*branding of the institution*". Additional pressures on institution-based staff (e.g. administrative duties, expectations of research, one-size-fits-all approach to teaching evaluation) are also cited as restricting space for creativity and preventing innovations in practice. Such experiences have led Nixon (2001b) to highlight the importance of the interplay of values at not only the individual and group practice level, but also at the organisational structures level. Therefore, during the integration of a performance-based organisation into a higher education institution, the areas of contestation emerging are largely grounded in a conflict between the values (and identity) of the institution, the discipline (including professional bodies and the wider industry) and those of the individual members of staff. However, as Nixon (2001a) notes, the accountability and reward systems in place in institutions is effectively strangling and reducing the space for academic freedom:

> A freedom that rebounds negatively upon those that try to exercise it is not particularly liberating. (p. 176)

The relationship between governmental and sector values may also be one to watch with the introduction of the Teaching Excellence Framework[2] and its planned discipline-level exercise. At the time of writing however this territory is charted, but not travelled.

Assessing the Performing Arts

All of the tensions emerging from the intersection between personal values and the values underpinning the broader context (i.e. disciplinary, institutional, sectorial etc.) are accentuated when considering how students' work are evaluated and assessed.

This section focuses on the potential impact of assessing the performing arts on both students and teachers. It considers how the continuous nature of performance lies in contrast to the testing culture that is the dominant discourse of higher education, and highlights the need for a shift towards an assessment for learning culture, which is perhaps the greatest area of tension faced by the performing arts.

The sheer breadth of assessment considerations within the performing arts can be problematic and influential throughout both a student's education and practitioners' academic careers. For instance, ever increasing grade requirements for students to enter university means that many strong performers are lost before A level grades are released. Anecdotal observation also indicates that with higher grades comes increasing levels of absence due to anxiety and depression. Perhaps these previously successful students A level assessment experiences lie in contrast to university level performing arts assessment? For example, one practitioner commented that "you have to be messy and precise to be a theatre designer", able to model-make, build sets, but also be able to work fluidly and reflexively, and handle complex ideas and conversations. However, this would appear to not fully align with institutional level testing culture, which is characterised by a focus on the quantifiable aspects of educational testing and synonymous with terms such as certification, measurement, outcomes and marking (Medland, 2016).

Whilst the testing culture is characterised by a focus on the product rather than the process of learning, performing arts performance projects (i.e. those activities that involve rehearsals which lead to a performance of some kind) can be assessed on the basis of either the process (i.e. the development and rehearsal of the performance) or the product (i.e. the performance itself). Indeed, many schools use a combination of the two; the assessment being weighted more towards process in the earlier parts of a student's training, and towards the final product in the later stages. Whilst both are subjective, this is not necessarily as problematic as the authors first assumed it might be. In conversation with practitioners, one of the greatest tensions seems to emerge when an institution "enforces standardisation which removes the discipline specific language". In other words, where generic grade descriptors appear disembodied from the subject being assessed. Thus, making explicit the differing levels of values at play that can create challenges. Greater harmony is often achieved where grade descriptors have been created as a means of "*translating*" university agreed standardised language into a discourse that is more appropriate to the nature of the performing arts, particularly in relation to the quality of the performance or process.

In view of the above examples from practice, the testing culture discourse is perhaps most visible within the quality assurance frameworks that have been implemented as a result of the massification of higher education in the UK, in an effort to codify standards and increase transparency (Bloxham, 2012). With specific lengths of units, credits, modes of assessment and regulations, the frameworks and structures of a university do not necessarily allow the flexibility needed for performance (see earlier discussion relating to the 15 credit module structure in place). Indeed, the "*organic interaction*" between practice and theory within performing arts disciplines, as one practitioner described it, would seem much more aligned to an assessment for learning culture, which is set in contrast to the testing culture, as its primary focus lies in the development of the learners as individuals and, therefore, the processes of learning. The call in the literature for a sector-wide shift towards an assessment for learning culture is arguably being threatened by entrenched techno-rational notions of measurement within quality assurance frameworks (Medland, 2016), and this is no more apparent than in the performing arts due, in part, to the inherently creative and perhaps more explicitly subjective nature of the discipline. However, whilst some clear challenges emerge from this potential for a disconnect between the values of the institution and those of the sector and individual educators, there is also a potential opportunity that emerges. A number of institutions are trying to mesh the quality assurance and learning and teaching elements to focus on enhancement rather than regulation. This could allow for the possibility of a lighter touch or more flexible approach to quality assurance that both maintains standards but allows the subject greater academic freedom. As a result, whilst the authors initially expected discourses surrounding assessment to be the primary focus of this chapter, the emergent organic conversations between us and with a range of performing arts colleagues, led to the identification of values and identity to be more influential in how the performing arts are perceived and enacted in practice.

The institutional focus on the products of assessment was referred to diversely by respondents as "mitigating against improvisation or being able to reward unanticipated learning outcomes". More than one noted the difficulty of asking students to explore and invent and then expect tutors to mark it. The bunching of assessments at the end of semesters was also described as being counter to the ongoing nature of performance. Furthermore, several respondents noted that a performance, being fleeting and then gone, is very difficult to assess, therefore you have to find other things to grade. This of itself is complex – a film of a performance is just a film, not the performance itself. If you are creating costume then the way the actors wear that costume may impact on the assessment of that item – another criticism being that you should not attribute the mistakes or successes of other (the wearer) to the designer of the garment itself. The difficulties here are, therefore, not necessarily firmly linked to a mismatch between assessment practices and institutional testing cultures, but perhaps more to do with the organisation, timetabling and logistics of designing assessment tasks that meet the institutional and sectorial expectations.

The collaborative and reflective aspects of elements and experiences of performance can be assessed but this generates thorny questions as to what an individual contribution may have been, how they have written about it and so forth. Assessment against learning outcomes, not least in institutions which have adopted maximum numbers per unit and argue for a certain kind of wording; to find that on certain performance units extensive numbers of short, specific learning outcomes to indicate exactly the aspect of craft that has been mastered, is out of step with the prevailing assessment philosophy. This juxtaposition between the dominant institutional testing culture discourse, and the creative disciplinary discourse dominant in the performing arts is perhaps why very little of the burgeoning assessment and feedback literature in HE has dealt with the performing arts context, combined potentially with the risks associated with articulating the misalignment between personal and institutional levels of values.

CONCLUSION

What is apparent from the preceding examples is that many factors can potentially derail the successful existence of performing arts courses in all their forms, but they have largely concentrated on the negative. Universities are by and large immensely proud of their theatres and their performance disciplines for the alternative, life enhancing contribution they make to a community. However, in certain universities (with the exception of specialist art and design institutions) this value and enjoyment of the performing arts may be a source of pride while also not necessarily sitting right up alongside other forms of learning and research. This may be due in part to the kinds of intelligences prioritised by the institution and the sorts of reputational aspirations it seeks. An institution which prides itself on its research performance, scientific predilections or espousal of traditional academic subjects may appear less interested in vocational or performative intelligences as opposed to more obviously academic or theoretical ones. It may shy away from making this apparent however, as theatres are attractive features of a university, not least for the popularity of their offerings. These can relate very strongly to commitments to offering an inclusive educational experience versus a competitive, selective elite model. While no university can afford to say it is anti-inclusive, the very nature of the demand for places on acting courses, for example, in ratio to those actually available inevitably means the successful candidate is in a position of privilege. In one college, 2,500 applicants compete yearly for 16 places on a course.

Conversations about the present day state of the performing arts voiced a number of concerns while also remaining upbeat, positive and resourceful as to ways of finding workarounds to systemic or regulatory barriers. Depending on the situation of the institution in question, different aspects of the debate were foregrounded – in one the clash between models of provision dominated, in another problems of assessment, in another a lack of understanding between the '*mothership*' (i.e. the institution) and the department on the receiving end of mainstream diktats as to how courses should operate which felt alien and unworkable to the course team. Another was jubilant as to the quality of the work that is being created and performed, irrespective of the negative elements at work, and another passionate about how the performing arts have a part to play in conjunction with every possible discipline. The deciding factor in these conversations appeared to come down to perceptions of success, trust, respect, value between institution and subject and relationships between all the different players on the pitch. The healthiest were inevitably where a genuine listening culture prevailed and there was room for negotiation and efforts to understand the opposing needs of the stakeholders in the game. Greatest negativity was found where morale had been eroded through an unbending attitude on the part of the most powerful players. For example, the existence of a blame and measurement/testing culture that failed to take into consideration the nuances of a subject area that has a rich history and significant potential to contribute to the life and identity of the university.

In view of the above, whilst the performing arts do not always fit neatly into the testing culture of broader institutional cultures, they are a distinct and valued part of what a university offers. In order for performing arts training in higher education to be successful there needs to be a balanced approach to assessment, testing of component skills, and knowledge and understanding in the early parts of training, moving towards an assessment model that recognises the complex and multidisciplinary nature of most of the disciplines that are subsumed within the performing arts. For this to happen, there needs to be a culture shift to one where the dominant perception is that art and arts form a significant contribution to the life and identity of the university, town and country. This must involve a sensitive and flexible approach to supporting cohabitation between different partners, perhaps through a lighter touch approach to quality assurance, which both maintains standards but allows for greater levels of academic freedom.

The extraordinary resilience and optimism in the face of challenges and contestation was a defining feature of the stakeholders involved, which was driven by a passion for the subject and an unwavering belief in its value. Practitioners also demonstrated a commitment to identifying solutions to the challenges faced by the performing arts that was grounded in a strong commitment to personal values and identity. However, support might usefully be applied to developing the perceived relationship between professional and pedagogical roles, so that practitioners view them as two sides of the same mutually beneficial coin, rather than in conflict. Furthermore, in view of the often tacit nature of ones values and identity, attention needs to be paid to the articulation of these elements so that resolutions might more easily be identified. This brings our chapter full circle back to the initial observation that Brexit and other political current affairs bring uncertainty about the value and identity of arts and cultural education in the UK. Stakeholders (including practitioners, educators, managers, researchers, professional bodies and institutions), therefore, need to work together to articulate the values and aspects of identity where commonalities and areas of contestation emerge so that the parallels and peculiarities between the performing arts and wider sector may be harnessed in meaningful ways.

NOTES

[1] The 15 credit module approach to curriculum design involves an institution operating a credit framework for all taught programmes based on a 15 credit tariff. All taught modules are 15 credits and the credit load for each year of a programme is distributed evenly over the academic year. An ordinary Bachelor's Degree requires the completion of 300 credits over the course of the programme.
[2] The Teaching Excellence Framework (TEF) is a Government initiative, which aims to recognise and reward excellent learning and teaching in England's universities: http://www.hefce.ac.uk/lt/tef/

REFERENCES

Becher, T., & Trowler, P. (2001). *Academic tribes and territories: Intellectual enquiry and the culture of disciplines* (2nd ed.). Buckingham: The Society for Research into Higher Education and Open University Press.
Biggs, J. (1999). What the student does: Teaching for enhanced learning. *Higher Education Research and Development, 18*(1), 57–75.
Bloxham, S. (2012). You can see the quality in front of your eyes: Grounding academic standards between rationality and interpretation. *Quality in Higher Education, 18*(2), 185–204.
Breakwell, G. M. (1986). *Coping with threatened identities*. London: Methuen & Co. Ltd.
Clegg, S. (2008). Academic identities under threat? *British Educational Research Journal, 34*(3), 329–345.
Collier, R. (2016, July 11). What will Brexit mean for arts and culture in the UK? *New Statesman* [online]. Retrieved November 7, 2016, from http://www.newstatesman.com/politics/brexit/2016/07/what-will-brexit-mean-arts-and-culture-uk
Harland, T., & Pickering, M. (2011). *Values in higher education*. London: Routledge.
Hemley, M. (2016, May 20). Nicholas Hytner: 'Free exchange of talent' will suffer if Britain leave the EU. *The Stage* [online]. Retrieved November 9, 2016, from https://www.thestage.co.uk/news/2016/nicholas-hytner-free-exchange-of-talent-will-suffer-if-britain-leaves-eu/
Macfarlane, B. (2004). *Teaching with integrity: The ethics of higher education practice*. London: RoutledgeFalmer.
Medland, E. (2016). Assessment in higher education: Drivers, barriers and directions for change in the UK. *Assessment & Evaluation in Higher Education, 41*(1), 81–96.
Nixon, J. (2001a). Not without dust and heat: The moral bases of the 'new' academic professionalism. *British Journal of Educational Studies, 49*(2), 173–186.
Nixon, J. (2001b). A new professionalism for higher education? In G. Nicholls (Ed.), *Professional development in higher education: New dimensions and directions* (pp. 73–88). London: Kogan Page.
Spelt, E. J. H., Biemans, H. J. A., Tobi, H., Lunung, P. A., & Mulder, M. (2009). Teaching and learning in interdisciplinary higher education: A systematic review. *Educational Psychology Review, 21*, 365–378.

Emma Medland
Department of Higher Education
University of Surrey
Guildford, UK

Alison James
Department of Academic Quality and Development
University of Winchester
Former Associate Dean of Learning and Teaching
London School of Fashion
London, UK

Niall Bailey
Guildford School of Acting
University of Surrey
Guildford, UK

IAN M. KINCHIN, MARTYN KINGSBURY
AND STEFAN YOSHI BUHMANN

4. RESEARCH AS PEDAGOGY IN ACADEMIC DEVELOPMENT

A Case Study

INTRODUCTION

This chapter reflects on the relationship between teaching and research as it may be conceived within a programme of academic/faculty development. A case study is presented of the interplay between a course participant, the course leader and the external examiner in terms of their complementary roles in navigating the research-teaching nexus.

Emerging models of academic development that focus on the structure of knowledge emphasize the need for a development of academics from *just* subject experts, towards professionals who can navigate the terrain between subject expertise and expert practice, and make this process tangible to their students (Behari-Leak & Williams, 2011). Such pedagogical abilities are seen to develop as a non-linear, iterative process, which needs to be finely balanced in order to protect academics' self-esteem and maintain their professional identities (Brody & Hadar, 2011; Hadar & Brody, 2017). The visualization of knowledge structures using concept maps was the focus of the dissertation that is at the heart of this case study (Buhmann, 2014), and offers a meta-lens to consider the teaching interactions that supported development of the dissertation. This supports explicit discussion of the trajectory of development, and requires academics to see pedagogy as an integral component of their disciplinary structure (Kinchin et al., 2017).

As university curricula draw increasingly on the research culture of the discipline (e.g. Varambhia, 2013; Werder, Thibou, & Kaufer, 2012), the stronger the argument becomes for strengthening the link between academic/faculty development and the disciplines, rather than maintaining a distance as a discrete, generic field. Viewing '*research as pedagogy*' (Dotterer, 2002) within academic development programmes helps link the scholarship of teaching more easily to academics' prior knowledge (that is based in the research of their discipline), and so allows academics to adopt a more scholarly approach to the pedagogy that underpins teaching, rather than adopt a surface (tips for teachers) approach to academic practice.

Within the examination process of university programmes, the role of the external examiner to provide independent scrutiny and quality assurance is considered fundamental to maintaining appropriate standards (Hannan & Silver, 2006), and has been considered as a leading example of '*best practice*' (Finch Review, 2011). However, the voice of the external examiner within this discourse is only now beginning to be studied as an influence on the process (e.g. Medland, 2015).

CONTEXT

Imperial College London is a leading research-intensive university with an international reputation for research and teaching within science, technology, engineering, mathematics, medicine and business (STEMMB) (QS, 2015; Times Higher Education, 2015). Much of the research and teaching at Imperial explores the interface between science, medicine, engineering and business. Students study with leaders in their field and benefit from opportunities created by the institution's strong industry relationships. The College is made up of four faculties: Medicine, Engineering, Natural Sciences and the Business School. There are no arts, humanities or social science departments, although some aspects of these areas are provided in a co-curricular study programme. The College is a member of the Russell Group of research-intensive universities and the majority of academic staff are research active; the institution's grant income in 2014–2015 was almost £367 million (Imperial College London, 2016). In the last Research Excellence Framework exercise over 90 per cent of College research activity was judged as '*world-leading*' or '*internationally excellent*'. Imperial College is then, a very STEMMB-focussed research intensive university.

Some have argued that such 'strong orientation towards research often reveal a weak emphasis on teaching and vice versa' (Gibbs, 2010, p. 29). However, while Imperial has a very strong research focus there is also an institutional commitment to offer a 'world-class education' (Imperial College London, 2013) and so the quality and training of teachers is also institutionally important. Training and support of university teachers, even in such a research intensive institutional context, is now established in the UK. This is, arguably, driven by league tables and the potential impact of student satisfaction, and by evidence that such training has a positive impact on both student learning and satisfaction (Gibbs & Coffey, 2004). Another motivation is the fact that even for students at Russell Group universities, having qualified teachers was their number one priority above professional expertise and research activity (HEPI-HEA, 2015). Such training varies between institutions but is often compulsory training linked to probationary requirements or tenure. However, this is not the approach adopted at Imperial, and the Master's programme considered in this case study sits within a spectrum of largely non-compulsory training and academic provision. This includes a suite of over thirty stand-alone workshops covering various aspects of teaching and learning and externally accredited CPD scheme leading to professional fellowship of the Higher Education Academy (HEA). The rationale for this approach is that, particularly in a research-intensive institution, during the initial probationary period when compulsory training is enforceable many academics are concentrating on establishing their research and consequently doing little or no teaching. This makes training in teaching less contextually relevant at best, and at worst, risks it being trivialised as an irritating administrative hurdle. The institutional strategy is therefore to make training flexible and freely available with as few potential administrative and process barriers as possible so that academics do the training according to need. While this tends to make the training more contextually relevant there is a risk that busy academics will avoid such training only seeking remedial support when in difficulty. Given Gibbs and Coffey's (2004) evidence that training and qualification in teaching improves student learning and experience, significant amounts of teaching to be performed by untrained and '*unqualified*' individuals is unacceptable.

As with all higher education institutions the academics are typically very busy, often with competing and conflicting demands on their time and having to make strategic decisions as to the priority of the various tasks required of them. Some will seek out educational training and qualification; teacher identity at research intensive universities can be complex and changeable (Skelton, 2012) with some academics seeing themselves as 'teaching specialists, blended professionals or researchers who teach' (p. 23). Those who have such views will tend to prioritise educational activity and engage regardless of compulsion or incentivisation. However, teaching exists in an academic prestige economy (Blackmore & Kandiko, 2011) that, particularly in research intensive institutions, holds research in the utmost regard, and others will prioritise their research activities over such training. In order to mitigate against inappropriate prioritisation and ensure that those teaching are trained and qualified the institutional approach is to try and ensure that training and qualification is more fairly balanced within this prestige economy. At an institutional level this means recognising and rewarding teaching expertise and qualification. In terms of the training and qualifications this means designing the provision such that participants '*value*' them. What this means in practice depends somewhat on the training, the stand-alone workshops need to be relevant and have pragmatic utility to participants, while the academic programme, such as the Master's under consideration here, need to not only be pragmatically useful, but also recognised as having academic integrity and merit.

One of the key things is that both the pragmatic training and the academic activity have to be '*authentic*' for those involved. A simple definition of such authenticity is difficult. Kreber et al. (2007, p. 40) suggest that authenticity is a '*multidimensional phenomenon*' aligned with 'being genuine, becoming more self-aware'. While Herrington and Herrington (2007, p. 68) describe authentic learning environments as being '*rich, relevant and real-world*', and authentic learning tasks as being '*complex, sustained and requiring intensive effort*'. In its simplest sense then, authenticity could be viewed as doing something '*for real*' but there are elements that go beyond situated learning in a '*real*' context and include elements of feeling '*real*' and appropriate. However defined, authenticity is desirable because learners engage better with more authentic, contextualised tasks (e.g. Herrington, 2006). In this case, this not only improves learning but by also linking the learning to need and context gives contextual '*value*' and '*personal prestige*'. In part then, the authenticity of training and support in teaching and learning arises from the being situated in a real context and from the perceived pragmatic utility of the content. In this sense such support and training could be considered to be '*work-based*' (e.g. Raelin, 2008) or '*work focussed*' (Powell, Millwood, & Tindal, 2008) learning. Both the Institutional and individual participant expectation for such training and support is of active engagement which is appropriate to a research-intensive context; although meaningful engagement means different things to different people at different stages of their careers (Blackmore & Blackwell, 2006).

THE ACADEMIC PROGRAMME

The challenge in this institutional context is to provide a range of flexible training, educational support and qualification for busy research-focussed STEMMB academics with situated authenticity such that they engage voluntarily to satisfy need and gain value rather than rely on compulsion. The nature of this challenge has significantly influenced the structure and approach to the Master's in Education (MEd) programme that forms the basis for this case-study. Imperial's MEd in '*University Learning and Teaching*' is a flexible, part-time programme with three stages. The first stage is a postgraduate certificate (PG Cert) that is situated in practice and consists of a core module of basic educational practice and theory and a choice of other modules related to the learning and teaching role and interests of the participants. For each module there is guided reading and face-to-face seminars that deliver and consider the theory and an assignment that requires the participant to link that theory to their context and practice. Each module assignment is given extensive formative feedback with the intention that this is used to reflect and integrate the various module assignments into practice and ultimately in a combined portfolio submitted at the end of the certificate for summative assessment. This first stage represents one third of the academic credit of the Master's, is assessed on a pass/fail basis for the academic credit and is also an accredited taught pathway to HEA Fellowship. This stage of the academic programme is strongly connected to the pragmatic authenticity of relating educational ideas to practice, but goes beyond the stand-alone training in that it is assessed and requires participants to be reflective practitioners by engaging in critical reflection upon their teaching practice. Participants can exit the programme at this stage with a PG Cert and fellowship of the HEA or they can gain HEA Fellowship and carry their academic credit forward and study for another year for a postgraduate Diploma (PG Dip).

The second stage (Diploma) is much more academic and research-focussed in nature and comprises two intensive taught weeks and a series of seminars that aims to teach participants (who are all research focused STEMMB academics) to engage critically with educational theory and literature. This is assessed with essays and with a substantial library project. The library project is supported by the seminars and by one-to-one supervision with three or four substantial supervision interactions and formative feedback on library project drafts at key stages. This PG Dip stage is a further one third of the academic credit of the Master's and is assessed towards the final graded Master's mark such that although the diploma is a pass/fail exit qualification marks are carried forward to the Master's which is graded pass, merit or distinction. In many ways, the PG Dip is the key transformative stage of the academic programme. It has a strong, rigorous academic authenticity requiring participants to think and behave as students of a new discipline. While the library project should be relevant to the participants' *'home'* discipline, at this stage it is important that participants critically engage with the literature and theory of education as novice students of education not simply as visiting *'experts'* from different disciplines. Without this authentic academic engagement with education as a new discipline there is a risk that the subsequent research project of the final Master's stage would be treated as a piece of positivist scientific research by the students who are, of course, all expert researchers in their primary scientific discipline. The aim of the PG Dip stage is therefore to give the participants the tools to critically engage with the literature and theory of education and to allow them to experience this as an authentic *'novice'* student in a new academic field rather than solely as an *'expert'* from another field. Participants can exit the programme at this stage with a PG Dip or they can carry their academic credit forward and study for another year for the Master's (MEd).

The final stage of this academic programme, the MEd, which forms the focus of this case study starts with an intensive week of face-to-face teaching and independent study that introduces participants to common educational research methods. While all the participants are expert researchers in their own scientific disciplines, educational research, particularly the qualitative approaches are new to them. As with the PG Dip, the taught component has a strong, rigorous academic authenticity requiring participants to think and behave as students of education. Following this week students have a period of self-directed study in order to conceive and present an educational research proposal based in a critical understanding of educational theory and if possible, relevant to their practice. Draft research proposals are considered in a mock ethics proposal process where participants role-play the part of reviewers and present and discuss their colleagues' proposals rather than present their own. This process, which is supported by the programme tutors, exposes the whole cohort to the range of proposed research and how multiple methods may be used and forms an initial check on the quality and scope of projects as potential MEd research. After this activity when the various project proposals and interests are established supervisors are assigned for ongoing one-to-one support based on interest and expertise.

From this point the authenticity and value of the activity changes so that, as far as possible, the research stage becomes an authentic research experience in education supported by the supervisor and a series of seminars at regular stages that offer opportunities for peer learning and support and give an awareness of a broader context. This approach has been designed to encourage and support participants in the use of their newly acquired educational research knowledge rather than simply utilising their existing scientific research expertise. However, where the research question demands or allows it appropriate quantitative or mixed methods can be used as long as they are supported by an appropriate educational rationale and theoretical grounding. Given that the participants are all experienced and effective researchers in their own scientific disciplines the scope and level of the research project often goes beyond what might normally be expected from students new to research working on a terminal academic qualification. While meaningful authentic educational research is not an academic requirement of the programme as such, it is often required to engage and challenge these participants. Figure 2 offers a visualisation of the academic programme and the MEd research project in the institutional context showing the relationships between some of the key components; particularly with regard to the institutional authenticity and prestige.

This chapter examines in some detail a case study where one such participant, an expert research academic from Physics combined his knowledge and experience of scientific research in a positivist physics paradigm with a thoughtful use of educational theory and approach to undertake some contextually relevant educational research to satisfy the requirements of his MEd studies. The authenticity of this as a piece of '*real*' and interesting educational research is indicated by its subsequent publication. This case study examines this final research stage as an example of pedagogy for academic development of STEMMB academics by considering the interplay of the dual roles of the actors involved as student & researcher, teacher & colleague and external examiner & editor.

CASE STUDY: EDUCATONAL RESEARCH PROJECT

In the following, we present our case study of a specific research project which was pursued by one of the authors as a student (SYB) under the guidance of a supervisor (MK) as part the Master's in Education (MEd) programme during the period September 2013 to July 2014. The third author (IMK) acted as external examiner to the programme.

Research Project

The project aimed to answer the question: can concept maps be used to reveal conceptual understanding of '*light*' of physics students at different stages of their education? To that end, 19 beginner (BSc) Physics students and 16 more advanced (MSc) Physics students at Imperial College London were asked to create a concept map (*sensu* Novak & Cañas, 2006, 2007) of their understanding of '*light*'. Three students from each of these samples were interviewed to verify central issues emerging from the analysis of these maps. In addition, the two leaders of the second-year Electromagnetism course were asked to produce an *'expert'* concept map during an interview session.

The concept maps were studied by means of quantitative, morphological and content analysis schemes which were developed as part of the project (Buhmann & Kingsbury, 2015). The findings were interpreted in terms of Ausubel, Novak, and Hanesian's (1978) theory of meaningful learning and within the framework of Nespor's (1994) chain of mobilisations. The main results of the project as reported by Buhmann (2014) include the developed framework for concept-map analysis which combines topological attributes and global morphologies; the observation that concept maps tend to become narrower and deeper for more advanced students without developing into true networks; an identification of manifestations of Ausubel, Novak, and Hanesian's (1978) five essential processes of meaningful learning in concept maps; and evidence that Nespor's (1994) chain of mobilisations is a good model for the web of abstractions constructed by physics students in the course of their learning trajectory.

Chronology

A brief overview over the chronology of the research project and its main stages is given in Table 1. To stress the student-supervisor relationship, forms of contact with the supervisor are indicated where applicable and week 0 is identified with the official start of the MEd. Hence, negative week labels indicate events taking place before this week. Breaks in study are indicated and are included in the week count, these reflect the part-time flexible nature of the MEd and not formal interruptions from the programme.

While the MEd ends on week 46 with the exam board, the week count is continued to give an indication of the chronology of writing and publishing the paper that originated from this work.

Student Account

In the following the student (SYB), provides his own personal account of the project. His reflections are split into pre-project, during-project and post-project stages.

Pre-project: initial motivations, choice of project and supervisor. My underlying motivation which influenced most decisions taken within the context of the project was to view the MEd programme as a chance for trying out a *'what if'* scenario. I had often been wondering what paths I could have followed as alternatives to a career in physics. So here was the chance to live and work as a member of a completely different field in a social science. Hence, I perceived the programme and my project as genuine research in its own right rather than a tool for enhancing my teaching practice in my native field of physics; I was aiming for an experience of legitimate participation in this new research community.

Table 1. Chronology of the research project

Week(s)	Stage/Event	Contact with supervisor
–2 – 0	*Preparation:* Decision for MEd programme, consideration of research ideas	Informal 1 – 1 meeting
0	*Start of MEd – taught week on research methods* *Background reading:* research ideas	Group & 1 – 1 teaching
1 – 2	*Preparation and submission of research proposal*	Proposal submission
3	*Allocation of supervisor*	Supervisor reviews research proposal
4	*Mock ethics panel*	Group seminar, Peer & supervisor feedback
3–7	*Refining research method* *Preparation of data gathering:* concept maps	1 – 1 supervisor meetings & phone conversations
10–12	*Literature search:* phenomenology + concept maps Preparation & submission of research ethics	1 – 1 supervisor meeting & phone conversations
12	*Ethics approval*	
12–14	*Data gathering:* concept maps	1 – 1 supervisor meeting
11–14	*Data analysis:* concept maps	1 – 1 supervisor meeting
11–12	*Preparation of data gathering:* interviews	Group seminar, 1 – 1 supervisor meeting
14	*Research update and review*	Group seminar, Peer & supervisor feedback
14–16	*Background reading:* interviews	
14–16	*Data gathering:* interviews	1 – 1 supervisor meetings
	Break in MEd research study	
22	*Research update and review*	Group seminar, Peer & supervisor feedback
23–26	*Thesis writing:* introduction, literature review *Data analysis:* interviews	Written feedback
	Break in MEd research study	
35–36	*Thesis writing:* methods	Phone conversation & written feedback
36–38	*Data analysis:* interviews	
36–38	*Thesis writing:* findings	Written feedback
38–39	*Thesis writing:* discussion, conclusions, abstract	Written feedback
39	*Thesis writing:* final version	Written feedback
40	*Thesis submission*	
46	*Exam Board*	
46–56	*Writing paper based on thesis*	Iterative collaboration & co-writing
56	*Submission of paper.*	
79	*Publication of paper (Buhman & Kingsbury, 2015)*	

The structure and aims of the programme as learning-theoretical research as opposed to a transferrable skills course aligned very well with this motivation: as it turned out, my initial situation when choosing a project was in many respects similar to that of a research student in my own native discipline. Like a physics student, I had a rough overview over the discipline and some of its main directions such as behaviourism, cognitivism and social constructivism (akin to theoretical vs. experimental physics) and key concepts and frameworks like communities of practice, threshold concepts, cognitive apprenticeship, concept maps (analogous perhaps to cosmology, quantum optics, cold atomic gases etc.). I had developed a rough intuition on which of these directions I found more interesting without being able to anticipate what it would be like to be working in these fields. Like a physics student before choosing his/her research project, I had tried out some essential methods and techniques such as interviews, questionnaires, concept-mapping within the protected space of taught sessions (similar to laboratory works and problem-solving tutorials in physics).

As a consequence, my choice of project also proceeded in a way that is very similar to the way a physics student would choose his/her project. I chose a direction/field about which I wanted to learn more, cognitivism, and an associated method which I liked using, concept-mapping. Some decisions were influenced by my relationship with my own disciplinary background: on the one hand, my desire to legitimately experience research outside my native discipline led me to use qualitative tools such as interviews, content-analysis and interpretative frameworks from social science and to combine a large number of these new methods. On the other hand, I decided to find a playing field that I am comfortable in by introducing tools from mathematics and physics into the concept-map analysis.

My choice of supervisor, MK, had organically evolved during the first two years of the programme. I had purposefully chosen him to be my supervisor for some written assignments. During those interactions, we had established a good student-supervisor relationship. In particular, I had witnessed that he could fulfil my personal supervision needs by: granting of student independence, help in structuring and defining the scope of projects, original input to the interpretation and implications of findings and an appreciation for the difficulties of natural scientists in making the transition into social science.

During project: interactions with supervisor. My interactions with my supervisor during the project were mainly triggered by myself making an appointment or sending an email. As evident from Table 1, they roughly fall into three thematic groups according to their temporal coherence, form and function: planning, interpretation and writing.

In the planning stage, prior to and immediately at the beginning of the project, I had three loosely spaced face-to-face meetings with my supervisor, who had not been officially assigned at this stage, and, for the first two meetings, also the head of the MEd programme. Those meetings mainly evolved around the choosing and defining of both project and research question. In particular, my supervisor provided input on possible methods of data gathering and possible scenarios or protocols. In addition, we had discussions around the purpose and anticipated outcomes of the project. As indicated by the spacing of these meetings, they were followed by long periods where I would reflect on the supervisor's input to allow the project to take shape.

With a well-defined project at hand, I organised the running of the data gathering sessions without requiring much help from my supervisor. A second set of four face-to-face meetings then revolved around the very core of the project: the interpretation of findings and some fine-tuning of the purpose and central questions of the project. During this stage, I perceived my supervisor as a senior research collaborator from a slightly different field, who was able to provide context and background from the literature; react to, discuss, and critically scrutinise my findings; and provide original input in the form of ideas, what-if questions and hypotheses. We used both discussions and graphical representations during this stage. Again, independence was the key in my view: I felt completely free to pursue those of his ideas which resonated with my own thinking and drop those that did not.

The last set of four interactions was concerned with the writing of the thesis. These largely assumed the form of email exchanges with the one exception of a phone conversation. My supervisor initially provided advice on the structuring and scope of the thesis and placed it into the broader context of possible later research. The writing itself was very structured where I would write a draft for a chapter, email it to my supervisor, receive written feedback and act on it. Again, my supervisor acted as a critical examiner of the hypotheses and interpretations. In addition, he guided my attention towards the '*so-what*' aspect of the project.

Post-project: impact of project after completion. The research project had effects on me both internally and externally. Internally, it has provided me with legitimate participation in the social sciences and learning theory in particular. This means that I can follow central arguments and developments in this field. In particular, I am able to engage in discussions with social scientists at the interdisciplinary Freiburg Institute for Advanced Studies of which I am currently a member. Such exchanges provide stimulating excursions into a different scientific community as a welcome interruption of my everyday work in physics. The impact on my teaching is rather indirect and proceeds in two ways: I have used concept maps, the central method of my project, during lecture series both as a diagnostic tool and a means to make the internal structure of the topic tangible to the students; and my reception of learning-theoretic publications may eventually trickle back into my own teaching practice.

Externally, the inclusion of a research project in the MEd programme has had a large impact. University Learning and Teaching programmes are typically viewed with suspicion by many colleagues from my own discipline, with the main criticisms being based on the assertion that they provide superficial and simplistic instructions which streamline teaching styles and are hence inferior to experience-based guidance by senior colleagues from within physics. By stressing the fact that the programme was academic and that it had a strong research basis, I was able to overcome these criticisms and gain respect for the programme. This legitimisation was further aided by the fact that my findings were published as a scholarly article in an education journal (Buhmann & Kingsbury, 2015).

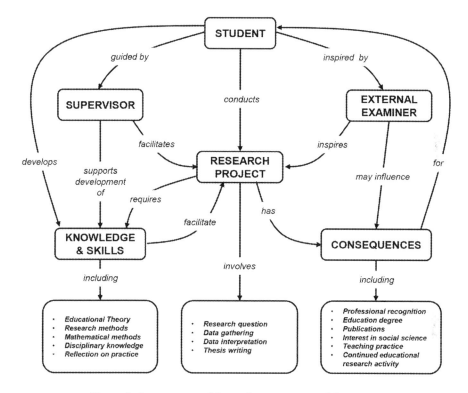

Figure 1. Concept map of the student perception of the process

The concept map in Figure 1 visualises the student's (SYB) own perception of the research project and the roles of the other two actors, the supervisor (MK) and the external examiner (IMK). The pre-project stage as represented in the lower left of the map mainly involved the developing of the necessary skills. With the exception of the disciplinary and mathematical knowledge, this was supported by the supervisor. In the during-project stage the knowledge and the skills were used to accomplish the steps listed in the lower centre of the map and the student made the transition from student to researcher. Here, the supervisor played a very active role as facilitator while the external examiner had an indirect influence by inspiring the chosen project with his research. The post-project stage involved the consequences listed in the lower right of the map. Here, the role of the supervisor shifted from teacher to colleague while the external examiner shifted his role to that of editor facilitating the publication of the scholarly article and hence cementing the shift in student transition to a researcher role.

Supervisor Account

In the following the supervisor (MK), provides a brief reflective commentary of the programme and the student's progression through the project. As with the previous section his reflections are split into pre-project, during-project and post-project stages.

Pre-project: Initial interactions during the PG cert and PG dip. While the final Master's stage is the focus of this case study I will start by briefly recapping my role in the transition from PG Cert through to the MEd, talking in general and highlighting specific interaction with the student (SYB). The PG Cert is a practice based stage with a pragmatic, situated authenticity that aims at engaging interested academics with educational ideas and helping them develop into more reflective practitioners. At this stage I teach modules on the research and teaching nexus and educational supervision, contribute to shared seminar activity, and undertake teaching observations. I also mark and second mark across the course. The student (SYB) was not my tutee at this stage and therefore I did not observe his teaching or mark his final portfolio submission, however he did attend one of my modules (educational supervision) and I taught him and gave formative feedback on his work. At this stage I see my role as helping students appreciate that there is an educational discipline that has a literature and theory that can be used to help them consider and improve their practice of teaching in their discipline. For some this is fairly superficial and while they use the literature to justify their existing views and/or gain hints and tips on teaching, they are not (yet) interested in education beyond that. However, many progress beyond this and start to understand that while the disciplinary content is their field of expertise there is another field, education, where they are less expert, that informs how their discipline is taught. This student, SYB, was interested in exploring education more and continued on to the Diploma stage.

At this stage I taught in the two taught weeks, facilitated in the seminars, marked essays and supervised and marked Diploma projects. I see my role during the Diploma stage as being much more academic by challenging the students to consider educational theory and critically engage with educational literature that goes beyond their disciplinary areas and expertise. Much of my effort is to help these bright academics, who are highly expert in their own STEMMB disciplinary areas, critically read and write in education (a Social Science) so they can then apply some of their existing disciplinary expertise and context to a consideration of this new field. Early in the PG Dip my role is to challenge students to engage, and support them through their early attempts at critical reading and writing to prepare them for critical engagement with educational theory and literature in the library project. During this they then need more '*distant*' supervision as they undertake self-directed study in a library project chosen by them to be relevant to their context. My role here is to help ensure the choice is appropriate and will meet the programme's academic requirements and to challenge thinking and encourage appropriate critical engagement. SYB was my PG Dip project student completing his library project *From threshold concepts to transformative learning: Cognitivist perspectives on how philosophy could enrich physics teaching*. He was a well-motivated, independent learner with a keen interest in education and we quickly developed an effective and, I hope, mutually rewarding student-supervisor relationship. This supervisory relationship led to informal preliminary discussions about possibilities for the MEd and possible research projects (as referred to in SYB's personal account).

During project: Interactions with student. My interactions with SYB as a student in the MEd are detailed in Table 1. At the very start of the MEd (weeks 0–3) my one-to-one was limited but I taught the group on the research methods teaching and facilitated the mock ethics review panel. Our more formal and focused one-to-one supervisions meetings started very promptly during week 3 when I was officially confirmed as SYB's supervisor. As I had already supervised him during the PG Dip our supervisory relationship was already well established and we had already had an effective way of working together. My approach to the supervision was to challenge and prompt at the start as the research question and methods were being considered and to be a foil to help SYB iteratively develop and take ownership of his research idea. I provided guidance as the ethics application was made but moved increasingly towards a more responsive stance as the project started the data collection and interpretation phase. During the writing up phase I took a traditional supervisory role offering critique of draft sections, trying to help SYB move beyond description and more superficial interpretation to think more deeply about his data and its meaning and use the critical skills he had developed in the PG Dip stage. My intention here was to provoke and guide, but to make it clear that the research was his. I also acted as a marker for the resulting MEd dissertation.

Post-project: Collaborating in a joint publication. After the MEd dissertation had been completed and marked and the full exam board procedures followed, SYB's enthusiasm and the quality of work and data was such that there seemed to be an opportunity to get the work published. This seemed to be a realistic possibility that fitted well with SYB's context and agenda, would benefit both of us as academics and would also bring 'value' to the programme given that peer reviewed research publication both indicates educational authenticity and a widely recognised academic prestige.

During this stage of the process my role transitioned from being supervisor, constrained by issues of assessment and teaching, to that of co-author. As co-author I was able to make more direct suggestions about data interpretation and presentation and to contribute to writing the paper in a way that would not have been appropriate for the MEd dissertation that the paper developed from. While the paper still represents SYB's work and he was lead author at this stage we collaborated as research colleagues. This represented a change in our professional relationship related to SYB's *'new'* status as a disciplinary expert of physics with authentic educational expertise. Ultimately this has led to the collaboration in this further scholarly work.

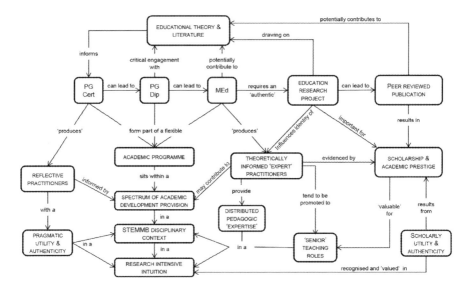

Figure 2. Concept map of the supervisor's perception of the process

EXAMINER'S REFLECTION ON THE PROCESS

One of the problems in linking teaching and research (in terms of quality assurance) is that the two activities often occur over different time-frames. The cycle of teaching on an academic programme is fixed by the institution and works on a clear annual cycle. Usually the teaching cycle is shorter than the research cycle and so outputs (such as publications) may develop some time after the programme has been completed. This delay results from the need for further reflection and development of the work based on feedback from the tutors, and also the speed of reviewing and editing to achieve publication in a journal. The work of external examining is typically inserted into the teaching cycle time-frame so that observations can be made before candidates are awarded their degrees, but engagement after the formal *'passing'* of a programme is likely to be ad hoc. Not only is the cycle of research typically longer than a year it is often less predictable – relying heavily on outside influences such as availability of peer reviewers who are not formal *'post holders'* in the way that an external examiner is, and on publication schedules that vary from one journal to another. The alignment of teaching and research cycles is therefore likely to be only serendipitous, such that the ability for the external examiner to have a meaningful role in linking teaching and research is restricted by a fragmented view of the overall process (with a focus around week 46 in Table 1).

The timing of the intervention of the external examiner usually occurs soon after submission of a thesis, before the implications or applications of the work can be fully realised. The thesis may, therefore, be seen as a '*work in progress*' even once the programme has been '*passed*'. The examination process is evaluating 'potential' to contribute to the research environment rather than a '*job done*'. Professional development can also be prolonged by delayed feedback of theoretical knowledge into e.g., teaching practice. In this case study, the timing of intervention by the external examiner hit a '*sweet spot*' when the developmental programme cycle and research cycle momentarily coincided for the student.

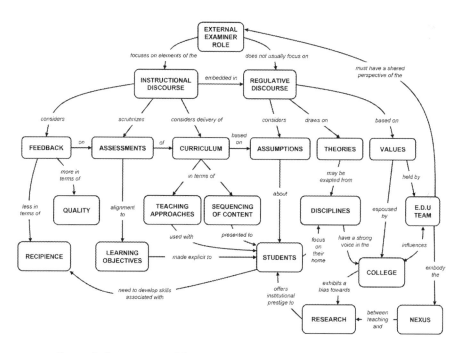

Figure 3. Concept map of the external examiner's perception of the process

Perpetuation of the separation of teaching and research may contribute to the development of pedagogic frailty within an institution (Kinchin et al., 2016; Hosein, 2017), with the result that academics feel more stressed than is necessary and feel inhibited in their teaching – persisting with conservative approaches to teaching practice (e.g. Canning, 2007).

Research outputs from the dissertation show the academic to be a producer rather than a consumer of education. This research activity adds authenticity to the academic development programme as it is seen to be engaged in the research environment that dominates the College – even though research that focusses on teaching or pedagogy has often been viewed as '*different*' to disciplinary research (e.g. Cotton, Miller, & Kneale, 2017). That a single programme participant has completed the cycle in this way, is an indicator that the process can work within the programme structure. The nature of the STEMMB academics engaged in this programme is such that around 20% will gain some sort of educational publication in the 18 months following the M.Ed. Mostly this will be in the form of a peer reviewed abstract with only one or two per cohort getting a full publication and often in a longer time-frame. From the external examiner perspective, it seems that the majority of the formal discussion required by the institution tends to focus on the instructional discourse that considers the mechanics of the teaching process rather than on the regulative discourse that considers the theories and values that underpin the teaching (Figure 3). There may be a tacit assumption that the examiner's value system is complementary to that held by members of the programme team. Variable timings of research outputs after the programme is completed mean that the external examiner is rarely able to observe the whole process, only fragments of it. This throws into question the timing of the examiner's intervention. In order to evaluate a programme on its research authenticity, then participation only in the examination board and QA activities of the instructional discourse closes down the dialogue before any research authenticity can be ascertained. Therefore, we have to infer from this that external examining is not designed to support a research-as-pedagogy model. This may provide an additional lens for the external examiner through which to observe the programme that may also observe more of the elements associated with regulative discourse (Figure 3). Additionally, if the external examiner is typically excluded from discussions about research outputs then they cannot either support or evaluate the workings of a research-as-pedagogy model of academic development. External examining may, therefore, be seen as a peculiarity of the system that simultaneously encourages innovation whilst maintaining a conservative approach to change.

IN CONCLUSION

Perhaps the key to using research as pedagogy in an academic development programme is that the research has to exhibit recognisable and robust authenticity, both as a way of integrating and often assessing the learning and also as research in its own right. This dual authenticity is especially valuable as academic development as it positions the pedagogy and education as research and scholarly activity that has easily recognisable academic prestige across the institution. This is true even in the research intensive, STEMMB focussed nature of the institution here. This is arguably of greater '*worth*' than the more pragmatic prestige associated with training and support for '*teaching*'. Exploration of this requires a long term relationship with the external examiner so that the actors involved may all be engaged in research-as-pedagogy. Whilst the programme described here is evidently able to successfully link research and pedagogy to produce authentic outcomes that are recognised by both teaching and research communities, the role of the external examiner needs to be tied into this approach if his/her influence is to have the same impact for the majority of students as it did in this case study.

REFERENCES

Ausubel, D. P., Novak, J. D., & Hanesian, H. (1978). *Educational psychology: A cognitive view* (2nd ed.). New York, NY: Holt, Rinehart and Winston.

Behari-Leak, K., & Williams, S. (2011). Crossing the threshold from discipline expert to discipline practitioner. *Alternation: Interdisciplinary Journal for the Study of the Arts and Humanities in Southern Africa, 18*(1), 4–27. Retrieved from http://alternation.ukzn.ac.za

Blackmore, P., & Blackwell, R. (2006). Strategic leadership in academic development. *Studies in Higher Education, 31*, 373–387.

Blackmore, P., & Kandiko, C. B. (2011). Motivation in academic life: A prestige economy. *Research in Post-Compulsory Education, 16*, 399–411.

Brody, D., & Hadar, L. (2011). I speak prose and I now know it: Personal development trajectories among teacher educators in a professional development community. *Teaching and Teacher Education, 27*, 1223–1234.

Buhmann, S. Y. (2014). *When 'light' dawns upon them: Mapping the essence of conceptual understanding of physics learners* (MEd dissertation). Imperial College London, London.

Buhmann, S. Y., & Kingsbury, M. (2015). A standardised, holistic framework for concept-map analysis combining topological attributes and global morphologies. *Knowledge Management & E-Learning, 7*(1), 20–35.

Canning, J. (2007). Pedagogy as a discipline: Emergence, sustainability and professionalization. *Teaching in Higher Education, 12*, 393–403.

Cotton, D. R. E., Miller, W., & Kneale, P. (2017). The Cinderella of academia: Is higher education pedagogic research undervalued in UK research assessment? *Studies in Higher Education*, 1–12. doi:10.1080/03075079.2016.1276549

Dotterer, R. L. (2002). Student-faculty collaborations, undergraduate research, and collaboration as an administrative model. *New Directions for Teaching and Learning, 90*, 81–89.

Finch Review. (2011). *Review of external examining arrangements in universities and colleges in the UK: Final report and recommendations*. Report commissioned by Universities UK and Guild HE. Retrieved from http://www.universitiesuk.ac.uk/highereducation/Documents/2011/ReviewOfExternalExaminingArrangements.pdf

Gibbs, G. (2010). *Dimensions of quality*. York: Higher Education Academy.

Gibbs, G., & Coffey, M., (2004). The impact of training of university teachers on their teaching skills, their approach to teaching and the approach to learning of their students. *Active Learning in Higher Education, 5*(1), 87–100.

Hadar, L., & Brody, D. (2017). Trajectories of pedagogic change: Learning and non-learning among faculty engaged in professional development projects. In I. M. Kinchin & N. E. Winstone (Eds.), *Pedagogic frailty and resilience in the university* (pp. 123–134). Rotterdam, The Netherlands: Sense Publishers.

Hannan, A., & Silver, H. (2006). On being an external examiner. *Studies in Higher Education, 31*(1), 57–69.

HEPI-HEA. (2015). *The student academic experience survey*. Retrieved from http://www.hepi.ac.uk/wp-content/uploads/2015/06/AS-PRINTED-HEA_HEPI_report_print4.pdf

Herrington, J. (2006). *Authentic e-learning in higher education: Design principles for authentic learning environments and tasks*. Keynote address, World Conference on E-learning in Corporate, Government, Healthcare and Higher Education, Chesapeake, Vancouver.

Herrington, A. J., & Herrington, J. A. (2007). What is an authentic learning environment?. In L. A. Tomei (Ed.), *Online and distance learning: Concepts, methodologies, tools, and applications* (pp. 68–77). Hershey, PA: Information Science Reference.

Hosein, A. (2017). The research-teaching nexus. In I. M. Kinchin & N. E. Winstone (Eds.), *Pedagogic frailty and resilience in the university* (pp. 135–149). Rotterdam, The Netherlands: Sense Publishers.

Imperial College London. (2013). *Imperial college London education and student strategy*. Retrieved from https://workspace.imperial.ac.uk/education-and-student-strategy/Public/Education%20Strategy_New_2013.pdf

Imperial College London. (2016). *Imperial college data and statistics*. Retrieved from http://www.imperial.ac.uk/about/introducing-imperial/facts-and-figures/college-data-and-statistics-catalogue/

Kinchin, I. M., Alpay, E., Curtis, K., Franklin, J., Rivers, C., & Winstone, N. E. (2016). Charting the elements of pedagogic frailty. *Educational Research, 58*(1), 1–23.

Kinchin, I. M., Hosein, A., Medland, E., Lygo-Baker, S., Warburton, S., Gash, D., Rees, R., Loughlin, C., Woods, R., Price, S., & Usherwood, S. (2017). Mapping the development of a new MA programme in higher education: Comparing private perceptions of a public endeavour. *Journal of Further and Higher Education, 41*(2), 155–171.

Kreber, C., Klampfleitner, M., McCune, V., Bayne, S., & Knottenbelt, M. (2007). What do you mean by "authentic"? A comparative review of the literature on conceptions of authenticity in teaching. *Adult Education Quarterly, 58*(1), 22–43.

Medland, E. (2015). Examining the assessment literacy of external examiners. *London Review of Education, 13*(3), 21–33.

Nespor, J. (1994). *Knowledge in motion: Space, time and curriculum in undergraduate physics and management*. London: RoutledgeFalmer.

Novak, J. D., & Cañas, A. J. (2006). The origins of concept maps and the continuing evolution of the tool. *Information Visualization Journal, 5*(3), 175–184.

Novak, J. D., & Cañas, A. J. (2007). Theoretical origins of concept maps, how to construct them, and uses in education. *Reflecting Education, 3*(1), 29–42.

Powell, S., Millwood, R., & Tindal, I. (2008). Developing technology-enhanced, work-focussed learning: A pattern language approach. In *Proceedings of special track on technology support for self-organised learners* (pp. 84–105). Salzburg: EduMedia.

QS. (2015). *QS world university rankings® 2015/2016*. Retrieved from http://www.topuniversities.com/university-rankings/world-university-rankings/2015#sorting=rank+region=+country=+faculty=+stars=false+search=

Raelin J. A. (2008). *Work-based learning: Bridging knowledge and action in the workplace* (2nd ed.). San Francisco, CA: Jossey-Bass.

Skelton, A. (2012). Teacher identities in a research-led institution: In the ascendancy or on the retreat? *British Educational Research Journal, 38*, 23–39.

Times Higher Education. (2015). *World university rankings 2014–2015*. Retrieved from https://www.timeshighereducation.com/world-university-rankings/2015/world-ranking#!/page/0/length/25/sort_by/rank/sort_order/asc/cols/stats

Varambhia, A. (2013). Perception of research-teaching links in natural and mathematical sciences. *Higher Education Research Network Journal, 6*, 75–82.

Werder, C., Thibou, S., & Kaufer, B. (2012). Students as co-inquirers: A requisite threshold concept in educational development. *Journal of Faculty Development, 26*(3), 34–38.

Ian M. Kinchin
Department of Higher Education
University of Surrey
Guildford, UK

Martyn Kingsbury
Educational Development Unit
Imperial College London
UK

Stefan Yoshi Buhmann
Institute of Physics
Albert Ludwigs University of Freiburg
Breisgau, Germany

ANESA HOSEIN AND JAMIE HARLE

5. THE VULNERABILITY OF A SMALL DISCIPLINE AND ITS SEARCH FOR APPROPRIATE PEDAGOGY

The Case of Medical Physics

INTRODUCTION

This chapter is based on a shared dialogue between an academic developer (first author) and a programme director of a Masters in Medical Physics (second author) who also sits on a professional external accrediting body for his discipline. This shared dialogue lasted about one hour in which the academic developer asked questions to the programme leader to aid in the co-construction of knowledge about the discipline by building on previous conversations we had together (see Dinkins, 2005). The academic developer directed the dialogue through questioning and prompting to explore and reflect on the programme director's understanding of the Medical Physics discipline within the United Kingdom (UK) and the challenges it faces with particular emphasis on pedagogy and how it may differ from other disciplines. The academic developer wrote the initial thematic interpretation of the shared dialogue which the programme director then responded and added to (which forms the basis of this chapter). This chapter, therefore, completes the shared interpretation of the dialogue when exploring the pedagogical peculiarities and challenges of the small discipline of Medical Physics – our case study.

We have taken a broad meaning to discipline in that we refer it to mean a particular academic subject area or field which has an established grouping of professionals/specialists in both academia and industry. Small disciplines can also be viewed as sub-disciplines which may be subsumed into a larger discipline(s). Therefore, Medical Physics is a small discipline which can be subsumed into either the larger healthcare science discipline (that encompasses all forms of scientific work completed in hospital settings) or into the physics discipline. One characteristic of the small disciplines is that there may be a small offering of programmes, that is, these specialist programmes are only taught at a few universities within a single country. As a consequence the number of student places offered, as well as the supply of disciplinary specialists to teach, is small. This low number of programmes can provide both opportunities and challenges with respect to appropriate pedagogy but this also places its search for appropriate pedagogies at possible risk or vulnerability. The pedagogical vulnerability we refer to here is possibly more likely for emerging disciplines. These small interdisciplinary subjects may be expected to comply with the pedagogical histories of the larger disciplines they belong to, which may provide tensions in how this small discipline approaches its pedagogical practice as well as how it searches, implements and establishes a new or emerging pedagogical practice for itself in the years ahead as it matures as an established university sub-discipline at the undergraduate and postgraduate levels.

Therefore, in this chapter, we do not propose the appropriate pedagogy for a particular programme, as there may not be a particular best pedagogy. Instead, we take the approach of focusing on what factors may affect the implementing of an appropriate pedagogy for the discipline. We will discuss the pedagogical challenges and peculiarities of Medical Physics within a UK context, based on mainly external factors. We take pedagogical challenges to be quite broad and encompassing both the learning, teaching, curriculum content and the learning environment.

CASE STUDY ON THE CHALLENGES: MEDICAL PHYSICS

Across the globe, Medical Physics is a sub-discipline that is pursued typically at postgraduate level by graduate scientists of several academic backgrounds, from computing to physics to technology, and also by those with an engineering first degree. The sub-discipline deals with applying physics and technological principles to medicine in order to diagnose, monitor or treat patients. Major subject areas within the sub-discipline include medical imaging (through technologies such as X-ray and computed tomography, magnetic resonance imaging (MRI) and ultrasound) and radiotherapy (which is radiation-based cancer treatment) as well as patient monitoring technologies (such as pulse oximetry). Within the UK, Medical Physics is delivered at around a dozen UK universities with many of the specialisms occurring at the postgraduate taught or masters level. Only a small percentage of university science students encounter Medical Physics during their undergraduate degree and only if their primary degree was in physics, where it is typically a pathway of a small subset of taught modules. In this section, we will explore the main issues and challenges that affect the pedagogy of the sub-discipline. These main issues formed areas of questions that the academic developer posed to the programme leader. These issues and challenges although presented separately influence each other.

Curriculum

In the UK, there are two main types of Medical Physics masters' programme, one is a three-year master's programme that is studied part-time at the university and the other is a one-year master's programme. The three-year master's programme has a significant clinical training component that is delivered within a teaching hospital when the student is not at university. This programme is aimed at meeting the workforce demand of the UK National Health Service (NHS) for hospital-based medical physicists. This three-year programme hence recruits almost exclusively from British or European Union (EU) students, as funding is provided for the three years for course fees and a trainee stipend by the NHS, on the expectation that the graduate would continue to remain a member of the NHS workforce at completion. The second type, the one-year master's programme is aimed primarily at the international student market, as well as UK or EU students aiming for a research career, albeit with part-time and flexi-time options for a small subset of students not able to study over 12 months full time, such as those already working in industry. In the three-year degree, the curriculum tends to be drawn from a healthcare science discipline perspective whilst in the one-year degree, it is drawn from a mainly physics perspective. Hence an appropriate pedagogical approach in these two programmes may differ as the student body, programme aims, graduate destinations and funding bodies covering tuition fees are essentially different. This section we will discuss how the types of programme and its curriculum content can affect the use of an appropriate pedagogy.

Types of programmes. In the NHS programme, students aim to become practising professionals upon graduation and hence the teaching is designed to ensure that students achieve the level of practice to be competent in the tasks required of them as qualified healthcare scientists in a hospital environment. There is a danger therefore that these programmes concentrate excessively on the practice of Medical Physics with a limited grounding in the theory. Indeed, many of the learning outcomes of such programmes are informally still referred to as "competencies" by the hospital staff that deliver some of the teaching. The use of competencies is a historical carry-over from the medical sciences' conventions and educational standards that matched the historical approach to training medical students, where young doctors would be expected to demonstrate competence in clinical procedures to pass practical or written assessments.

Further, these programmes may not focus on developing students' higher levels of thinking skills such as evaluating and creating (see Biggs, 1999; Bloom, 1956; Krathwohl, 2002). The pedagogical approach in this three-year Medical Physics programme is often delivered in a risk-averse manner that discourages innovation, creative thinking or other forms of original application or modification or technology which may result in non-compliance with radiation or health and safety laws. The reason for this is that these medical physics students are not expected to experiment and try different methods as there are fixed clinical protocols in hospitals. Indeed, clinical protocols are often written to ensure that a practising healthcare scientist stays within a host of legislative limits and efficacy standards for diagnosis or treatment. As an example, marking descriptors in NHS programmes can typically define a fail mark (<50%) as *"containing unsafe practice"*, and this can restrict students from being offered innovative or creative work in their assessments. Hence, the pedagogical approaches do not often encourage students to use their knowledge in different ways i.e. having extended abstract thinking (Biggs, 1999), and instead, tend to emphasise a protocol-based approach to work that can stifle creativity and innovation.

In contrast, because of its short duration, the one-year masters may be in danger of '*churning out*' masters graduates without allowing students adequate reflection time to encourage a deep approach to learning, that is, there is little room in the curriculum to enable students to make connections (i.e. relational knowledge) between the different concepts they are learning in the various modules of their degree (Entwistle & Tait, 1990; Gow & Kember, 1990). It is possible that this curriculum may encourage a pedagogical approach that enables atomistic thinking, that is, discrete blocks of learning. These issues are not peculiar to this one-year masters but to all programmes in this format. Further, with the cohort primarily being international students, they may have specific expectations of how teaching should occur and any departure from these expectations may take a period of adjustment which may not be possible in a one-year master's degree. For example, some international students may expect a pedagogical approach that is mainly didactic such as a lecture-based approach (see for example Huang, 2005; Vu & Doyle, 2014). If, however, the pedagogical approach was more active such as in problem-based learning, this different approach may require introductory sessions where students have to practice and adjust to problem-based learning (see Drake, Hovmand, Jonson-Reid, & Zayas, 2007). However, there may not be space in the curriculum for this adjustment in a year, particularly in programmes that are modular, and typically delivered over a university term/semester of 12 weeks. Further, compounding the challenge of selecting an active learning pedagogical approach is that international students whose first language is not English may feel uncomfortable in an active learning environment where the defence of the thought processes and discussion of newly-established ideas among peers requires a quick and confident command of the English language (see for example Vu & Doyle, 2014). In addition, they may require a confidence to introduce and defend ideas, some of which may be non-conventional, speculative or counter-intuitive, and which may be easily argued against by peers, or the key breakthrough in ideas development by the group. This effect may be compounded by group behaviours in such collaborative activities, as performance in early tasks is essential to an individual defining their most effective role in a group task, developing skills needed to successfully collaborate, and building the confidence to suggest those creative ideas that are quickly rejected or adopted by the group. Considering these highlighted issues with using active learning approaches, some one-year programme leaders may consider the didactic approach as being most parsimonious.

On the Medical Physics one-year masters, learning is almost exclusively in a university environment with one or two major assessment periods. The students on these programmes tend to be assessment-focused in their learning aims. In comparison, on the three-year NHS programme, the assessment also takes place during students' hospital duties on a regular basis. These NHS-supported masters students adopt a more integrated approach to learning where taught content from university modules and hospital practice can be synthesised to demonstrate the meeting of the learning outcomes using a variety of assessments: some university-based and some in the hospital settings. As a result, three-year students may take a more formative approach to each individual assessment, as learning from the assessment feedback can improve future performance, and each assessment is a *'small stakes'* component of their overall mark. For one-year university students, the assessment process is certainly more summative in outlook; one or two assessment periods make assessment scores *'high stakes'* and students are often denied the opportunity for individual feedback, if the assessments were exam-based, which can enhance their future performance.

As the discipline is small, and these two types of Medical Physics curriculum have distinct well-evolved approaches, there is a level of protectionism of each pedagogical approach. This can create issues in the accreditation of all Medical Physics programmes through a joint framework that evaluates the educational standards and learning environment of all programmes. For example, accreditation assessors for both of these Medical Physics programmes who undergo training before their work are recruited from both types of programme to complete an assessment report for the accreditation panel on a programme from the other distinct programme. In short, those familiar with the three-year programme often criticise the one-year programmes for lacking sufficient clinical application and for being too assessment-focused, while those from the one-year masters find the NHS programme lacking in opportunities for students to show critical thinking, as well as being short on insight into recent innovations in the sub-discipline. Thus in this small discipline pedagogical change can be hard to implement and viewed with distrust as it encroaches on the two different Medical Physics identities (that is of practice vs theory and research).

Curriculum content. Due to its interdisciplinary nature, the Medical Physics master's programmes tend to draw on students from various undergraduate disciplines such as mathematics, physics, engineering, computer science, and occasionally medicine or biological sciences. This raises issues in how the programme is taught in that the curriculum has to accommodate a diverse knowledge background of the students. Sometimes in the master programmes, this accommodation is not made and students are expected to have knowledge of the cognate discipline and students have to fill in this lack in their information for themselves. This, however, can lead to fragmented (Crawford, Gordon, Nicholas, & Prosser, 1998) and surface learning (Marton & Säljö, 1976) by students as their main aim is to recollect in exam conditions the information required for passing the assessments in topics in which they have a poor underlying background knowledge (Watkins, Dahlin, & Ekholm, 2005). Further, a tension arises within the discipline because of the two identities of what a medical physicist is, and what skills the students need to acquire to develop into a professional within one of these two identities. In particular, the NHS programme does not focus so much on relational or extended abstract thinking applied to the underpinning scientific theory of Medical Physics as their focus is on the application of knowledge to hospital work, particularly protocol-driven hospital work. In contrast, the one-year programme has a deeper focus on underpinning theory, as these programmes are often required to prepare students for research careers where skills such as mathematical modelling and hypothesis generation are essential for success in doctoral work.

This distinct approach by both types of programmes is unsurprising as different disciplines that have modules on similar topics often focus on different areas, for example, the teaching of linear programming in the soft disciplines (such as business and management) versus in the hard disciplines (such as in mathematics and operations research) concentrate on the applied instead of the pure aspects of the discipline. The soft disciplines in linear programming concentrate on the applying of the mathematical principles and use very little mathematics whilst the hard disciplines concentrate on understanding the underlying theoretical/mathematics principles – the pure aspect of the topic (Hosein, 2005). Using this hard/soft and pure/applied classification (Biglan, 1973a, 1973b) based on how the discipline uses knowledge, the Medical Physics programmes can be classified into two types of sub-disciplines: a hard-applied discipline (NHS programme) and a hard-pure discipline (one-year master). Therefore, this emerging small discipline as it tries to find its position may be subjected to disciplinary fracturing in terms of whether it should be pure or applied and this disciplinary position can affect its pedagogical approach.

This pedagogical disciplinary fracturing is further seen where the NHS programme concentrates on the teaching of the routine use of bespoke medical equipment according to clinical protocols, that is, the applied aspect of Medical Physics. However, the teaching about bespoke equipment has little relevance for international students who would not have access to some of the specialty medical equipment in their home countries (such as linear or proton beam accelerators) or research scientists, who would need to have the theoretical grounding to apply the knowledge to their context, and indeed are looking to further develop the technology in their future work, rather than correctly apply the technology to clinical practice. This suggests where there are different foci based on how groups view their discipline, this can affect the curriculum and may cause conflict on the appropriate pedagogical approaches.

Trained Teachers

One of the other issues that arise from being a small, emerging discipline is having sufficiently trained Medical Physics teachers in higher education theory and practice. Within the UK higher education sector, early career academics are encouraged to become trained teaching professionals usually by taking a postgraduate certificate in academic practice that is recognised by the UK Higher Education Academy (HEA). However, within the Medical Physics discipline, the number of teachers with this qualification is quite low. A survey of accreditation paperwork across eight UK masters programmes by the second author indicates that teaching qualifications are held by only around 10% of those who teach on Medical Physics master's programmes. There are a number of reasons for this. Firstly there is not a large pool of Medical Physics professionals who are willing to teach or become academics, as the vast majority are employed in the NHS or private hospital sector, where there is little career reward, funding or day release for completing this postgraduate certificate. Therefore, the teachers tend to be guest lecturers drawn from industry or hospitals on an *ad hoc* basis who may not have the time or the inclination to undertake an additional qualification in training to teach. Secondly, there is a lack of awareness of the teaching qualification within the small sub-discipline, and since few teaching staff hold it, there is no inclination by universities to include it in job descriptions of career promotion gateways. Thirdly, with a small number of programmes per country, career progression in teaching specialist roles can be non-linear, with opportunities dependent on the retirement of existing staff, and the creation of new posts often on a part-time basis initially while the emerging sub-discipline grows.

In the UK, the recently launched Teaching Excellence Framework (TEF) for Higher Education is designed to provide information for fee-paying students on the quality of their higher education learning experience, with the ultimate aim of the UK government being to raise sector-wide standards and prestige in an institution's teaching quality. The Medical Physics sub-discipline, with its low rate of teachers holding formal teaching qualifications, may suffer relative to other disciplines and sub-disciplines in the teaching metrics for this assessment exercise.

Further, as teaching is a duty that the guest lecturers undertake in addition to their normal job, there is little guarantee that there will be a sufficient number of lecturers in any given year and hence the programme leader has to lobby and negotiate with these professionals to provide lectures. The content of these lectures can be variable, and even repetitive if several guest lecturers are used, and tend to be based on the professional's own experience and related to the practicalities of how they accomplish their jobs. Hence the guest lectures on some occasions may not have aligned learning outcomes to the programme, lack a coherent lesson plan and do not challenge students in their higher levels of thinking. In fact, very few lecturers in Medical Physics may be aware of the learning outcomes approach which forms the basis of constructive alignment theory (Biggs, 1996) that has been advocated across the UK higher education sector. Their teaching may be often content-driven and primarily based on the practical side of their profession. Hence, whilst students may be able to acquire good insights into the practical side of the profession, the standard of lectures required for meeting master's level thinking may be variable.

For example, guest lecturers are invited in to teach a particular topic/content. As these guest lecturers may not meet as a team and decide how each lecture links to each other, the lectures are instead a series of topic areas without any forward and backwards linkages. Thus lectures are often stand-alone with the expectation that students will be able to find the relational links between the lectures. This pedagogical approach may promote students learning using a surface approach, that is, learning discrete information rather than relating the information. Therefore, small emerging disciplines face the challenges of ensuring they have qualified and trained personnel for their programmes as well as trying to meet the required higher education metrics such a sufficient number of trained/qualified teachers.

Job Market

This section looks at two aspects of the Medical Physics discipline job market. First is, for the degree programme to meet the needs of the student and the sector in terms of employability. The second aspect looks at how the small number of jobs in the discipline affects the expansion of the programme.

Employability. The role of the degree in higher education is changing, in particular, students are more likely to emphasise that the degree provides them with a high level of employability (Diamond, Vorley, Roberts, & Jones, 2012). On the flip side, employers want students with certain attributes that fit with their industry (see Hinchliffe & Jolly, 2011). Although Medical Physics is a small discipline, due to its interdisciplinary nature, the degree has to meet the needs of several career fields. Notably, there may be a disparity between the NHS programmes and the one-year programmes on the type of employer engagement, which is also one of the TEF measures. Teachers on the NHS programmes will likely concentrate on developing a curriculum which shows excellent engagement with a single established national employer, namely the NHS, while the teachers on the one-year programme curriculum will engage with industry, research groups and small to medium enterprises that foster future innovation. It remains to be seen whether engagement with established employers, which are part of the existing fabric of the UK healthcare sector or with innovation and technology companies, that are often seen as the driver of future economic growth, from the favourable employers is where engagement should be focussed.

Therefore, the main job markets for the degree is within the clinical setting (i.e. working in hospitals), working within research (including higher education and research laboratories) and in the industry (such as medical equipment manufacturers in multinational or small to medium enterprises). In addition, students may seek employability in other related areas such as with regulatory authorities, science education or science communication. Considering the job market, the Medical Physics degree programme leader faces a strain in developing a curriculum that ensures that all students are able to follow these career paths. The clinical field needs students who are skilled in the safe use of complex medical technology whilst the research field wishes to recruit students who are able to critically think and perform research to advance the applications and efficacy of patient treatment, diagnosis or monitoring. Learning outcomes in the degree that favour one aspect over another may create a frustration amongst students who have a particular employment path in mind. If students' extrinsic motivation for reading the Medical Physics degree is for a particular employment/occupational track, this may lead to high levels of student dissatisfaction in certain course content areas as students may view some content as being superfluous to their needs.

Contributing to this issue of employment is that international students will also want the Medical Physics qualification to be portable to their country, that is, the degree needs to be relevant to their national context. This raises issues where content within the Medical Physics degree is inevitably Anglo-centric, with study materials and assessment addressing aspects of legislation and clinical protocols that relate to UK or EU law or guidance that is not applicable or consistent with the guidance in other countries. Inevitably, this legislation will be different or non-existent in some countries and international students may find this aspect of the teaching not relevant to their likely employment route back in their home country. The counter-argument, which some students will accept, is that UK/EU standards are often among the highest in the world and that a master's level education should enable students to tease out the reasons why different legislative approaches are in place in different countries. However, overseas funding bodies and employers can often fail to recognise this new skill of relational thinking in terms of understanding why laws and practices vary across the globe, particularly in hospital environments where the practice is protocol-based, and a more uni-structural or multi-structural thinking to perform clinical duties with competence is sought by employers (Biggs & Tang, 2007).

The peculiar way in which the degrees have been *'farmed out'* to different sectors (NHS and Higher Education) is one way that the discipline has ensured the stakeholders' needs are met. This, however, means that the student has to be clear before starting their degree into which sector they wish to continue as there may be little room for cross-over after graduation as their different learning experiences train them towards different employment routes.

Small employment sector. The Medical Physics discipline has a finite number of professionals that are needed in the sector. The UK NHS has around 3,000 medical physicists employed at any point. Further, as with most disciplines, the number of Medical Physics students who go onto research within higher education is dictated by the research funds available. Researching Medical Physics in higher education institutions is focused on a small number of UK universities as it depends on the institution having access to expensive equipment, a research partnership with a large teaching hospital and a critical mass of staff with an academic track record. As research funds from the UK government become increasingly targeted to leading institutions with high performance in its research audit process, known as the Research Excellence Framework, the universities that offer Medical Physics at masters and doctorate level are ones with already established research centres and laboratories. These research centres will only recruit the number of research students that they have successfully acquired funding for postgraduate study and hence this number can be dependent on the vagaries and instabilities of the grant funding process. This is more so as physics-based cancer treatments continue to compete for clinical effectiveness against emerging lab-based biological treatments such as immunotherapy and chemotherapy. This leads to periodic changes in national strategic funding priority as to how cancer research is funded between physical and biological techniques, with one approach periodically making a breakthrough that shows preference over the other, albeit temporarily.

Within the industrial sector, there are only a few specialist companies that deal with the development and testing of Medical Physics equipment, although this is a growing field due to the emergence of biomedical engineering as a new engineering sub-discipline in which medical devices are designed for even more diagnostic applications. Industrial sectors, however, have a preference for recruiting staff with existing industrial experience, and this is an acute trend within Small to Medium enterprises (SMEs), where a new recruit may be expected to take on multiple company roles as well as manage projects. This favours industrial recruitment away from the fresh graduate in Medical Physics and leads to a small number of first-job opportunities for new graduates, normally within the larger multinational companies of the sector, where a structured and supervised programme of postgraduate training can be implemented (Wakeham, 2016).

This means that the expansion of degree programmes are limited by the potential number of students. The number of students who would opt for a Medical Physics programme, in theory, is not limitless. Hence, programme leaders are competing for the same applicants for programmes. This competition becomes particularly fierce where universities are asking programme leaders to increase the number of the students in order for their programmes to be financially viable. Therefore, the master's programme may have to differentiate themselves from other programmes in the way they are taught and delivered. This, however, may create an atmosphere of secrecy and non-sharing of pedagogical practices within the Medical Physics discipline. In addition, due to the small number of students usually on a programme, the programmes may be vulnerable to being closed down should cohort numbers fall below numerical thresholds set by each university. Although not particular to this programme, the programme leaders may be more tempted to use pedagogical practices that are '*tried and tested*', such as lectures, rather than innovative practices which may be '*hit or miss*' when it comes to student satisfaction evaluations. This matter is also relevant for international students, as overseas governments funding the programme for its students may expect a traditional didactic approach on how a programme's educational content should be delivered, and so express concern at more contemporary forms of teaching delivery, like problem-based learning or other active methods.

Validation and Accreditation

This section looks at how the processes of validations and accreditations can affect the small discipline. Two issues are examined, firstly the need and the use of external examiners and secondly when accreditation processes are changed.

External examiners. The higher education Medical Physics sector is small and the pool of experienced external examiners is also small. This means there is unlikely to be an expansion of new programmes at other universities; hence Medical Physics programmes are likely to be only at the universities with a proven track record. This presents a challenge when programmes have to be re-validated and re-accredited by their university and professional, statutory, or research bodies (PSRB) respectively. The issue here is that the Medical Physics academic community being small may sometimes find it difficult to obtain external examiners for their validation panels who do not have some link with the programmes across the country. This sometimes can lead to nepotism within the discipline; where a few persons who are leaders in the discipline control how the discipline and its curriculum is shaped in the future. Further, there can be sometimes issues in objectivity in the validation process as the programmes need to compete with each other and there may be unconscious bias in providing advice that helps a rival programme develop and improve its educational product.

The challenge, therefore, is fostering a climate where junior academic staff are able to shape the future of the discipline as well as ensuring that biases are acknowledged and that academics are able to negotiate ways of sharing and building on others' pedagogy without sacrificing their competitive edge.

Changes in the accreditation process. In addition, the accreditation by PSRBs also affects how these programmes are taught. Within Medical Physics, in the UK, there are two main PSRBs for the master's programme, the National School for Healthcare Science, which accredits solely the NHS master's programme and the Institute of Physics and Engineering in Medicine (IPEM) which accredits both masters' programmes. As the PSRBs have particular motives in mind on how they would like the discipline to develop this influences the curriculum and hence the pedagogy of the discipline. This is not different from any other discipline which is subjected to its PSRB requirements. Recently, IPEM overhauled its accreditation process moving from a syllabus-based to a learning outcomes approach. These changes in the accreditation process, therefore, means that programmes have to now change their current offerings to align with IPEM expectations. However, this can affect degree programmes as they may have to ensure that they have the qualified personnel and/or equipment to ensure the new learning outcomes can be achieved.

Changes in accreditation policies make a small discipline vulnerable as some programmes may have limited flexibility to accommodate the pedagogical changes within its programme in terms of time, staff and equipment. Therefore, the challenge for this discipline is ensuring that there is continuous dialogue between itself and its PSRB as to be aware of the expected direction and changes to ensure these can be adapted gradually into current programme offerings.

League Tables

The last external issue that is considered here is that of league tables. In the UK, all undergraduate programmes are ranked by their National Student Satisfaction (NSS) scores. However, at the postgraduate level, there is an optional survey known as the Postgraduate Taught Experience Survey (PTES). The Medical Physics discipline is aware that it is likely the PTES (or a similar survey) may become compulsory across the postgraduate sector. This has implications for the Medical Physics programmes on some of the issues raised previously on the competition of recruiting students. Each programme within the Medical Physics discipline is hence trying to ensure their students are satisfied with the degree programme so that impressive PTES scores will result. These Medical Physics programmes will want to be consistent with other programmes and not show clear discrepancies so that students feel unsure of what the programme is delivering. Innovative pedagogy can suffer when programmes wish to remain with pedagogies that have worked before.

Within the one-year master's degree, particularly those in more established research (or prestigious) centres, a tension begins to arise where teaching is aimed at ensuring student satisfaction. An attitude of '*sink or swim*' (that is, pass or fail based on only one's effort) may pervade in these institutions in which it expects students to be independent learners with limited support and feedback from the lecturer as they are being trained to be the next independent researchers. However, this attitude does not lend itself to ensuring high scores in student satisfaction surveys particularly as support and feedback are rated as very important by students in such surveys. It is also unpopular with international students who feel they have to adapt to the new living and learning cultures of the UK in addition to the studying requirements and may find the demands of requiring independent manner without close support unfair (Huang, 2005; Vu & Doyle, 2014). These departments may face some pressure between differing teaching staff who may feel that some lecturers are pandering to students to ensure that they have good satisfaction scores rather than acquiring the best students.

With the need to do better on league tables, there may be more of a tendency to perhaps compromise these teaching beliefs which can cause subversion in the teaching practices. As many of the Medical Physics teaching staff are not currently trained teachers, the discipline can take the opportunity of helping their teaching staff to find ways in which their teaching beliefs can still be upheld to some extent within a framework of support and feedback. However, as league tables may look to monitor the status of teaching staff at UK universities, there may be a further subversion if these staff are '*forced*' to undertake pedagogical training.

The challenge therefore within this small discipline is to train staff to implement an appropriate pedagogy that enables independent learning but at the same time ensures that students feel supported within that environment. In addition, careful consideration of course design, student support and preparatory resources may be needed to ensure that students feel comfortable and appropriately introduced to the pedagogical approach.

OVERCOMING THE CHALLENGES

In this chapter, we have identified through the dialogue of the programme leader and the academic developer, the challenges faced by a small emerging interdisciplinary discipline with respect to implementing and developing its pedagogy. These challenges are listed in Table 1.

Table 1. Challenges faced by the medical physics discipline in establishing appropriate pedagogies

Challenges
1. Encroachment of Medical Physics Identity
2. Fracturing of Discipline
3. Qualified and Trained Personnel
4. Wide Spectrum Degree for Employability
5. Reluctance in Sharing of Practice
6. Nepotism in Shaping the Discipline
7. Vulnerability to Changes by External Bodies
8. Meeting the Needs of Students

In this section, we will explore various ways in which these challenges can be addressed. We offer solutions to these challenges, however, these solutions are not definitive but instead are alternatives that the discipline may want to consider as it moves forward in the search and acquiring of an appropriate pedagogical approach. It is possible that these solutions can be used in other small disciplines as these challenges may not be peculiar to this discipline alone.

Issues 1 and 2: Identity and Fracturing

The first two issues in Table 1 are linked in that there are generally two main identities of the medical physicist; that of a healthcare scientist in a hospital and the other as a researcher or device specialist in the industry. These identities, in turn, lead to the fracturing of the discipline in that it is being pulled in two directions to align with these main identities. This fracturing of the discipline leads to different focuses in the pedagogical approaches. This is not an easy challenge to address. However, if these two branches of the disciplines are expected to use pedagogies that will raise the quality of their programmes, they need to establish their remit clearly and determine where they are different in terms of the intended skills development and curriculum and where there are similarities. Without this clear remit, it is likely that further fracturing of the discipline may occur and the pedagogies used may be atomistic rather than holistic. The fracturing may confuse and alienate their intended students and place their taught programmes in jeopardy.

Issue 3: Qualified and Trained Personnel

With respect to qualified and trained personnel, the Medical Physics discipline faces an issue with having a large number of non-academic guest lecturers. It is important for a discipline finding an appropriate pedagogy that these guest lecturers are trained in pedagogical practices to ensure that students have a consistent learning experience. This is a problematic undertaking as the non-academic guest lecturers are busy professionals who may be working in demanding hospital or industrial roles. It is unlikely that these lecturers will want to work towards a formal teaching certificate, or that their employer would offer the funding or day release to complete such studies. However, training can be put into place to allow these guest lecturers to at least earn a lower qualification that enables some pedagogical training, but without the required study hours or level of assessment output. Guest lecturers should still be able to reflect on the teaching they are currently undertaking. This training could be a pre-requisite or co-requisite of their teaching. Although the training may act as a detractor to some of the guest lecturers, appropriate pedagogies are unlikely to be developed from these guest lecturers spontaneously. If the training can be made flexible such as in an online environment and be linked to their payment or career recognition, such as Continued Professional Development activity or Chartered status, which many industry and hospital professionals require for indemnity or status reasons, it is likely that the number of qualified personnel can increase. This training would not only have a positive impact on the discipline in the league tables but move the discipline closer to implement appropriate pedagogies.

Issue 4: Employability from Degree

The need for the programme to train students that have employability in the wide spectrum of Medical Physics jobs is linked to challenges one and two, in that the fracturing of the discipline determines which employment route is focused on. If the remits of the disciplinary identities are clear, then students may be able to make better decisions. If students wish to cross-over there should be provided with the opportunity to top-up modules that allow either clinical training or research-based training. However, given the small number of students, this should ideally be offered from one institution but without the need to be in a specific geographic location. Furthermore, both degrees should ensure that it allows students to have a high level of critical thinking as the types of employment roles in the sector require considerable amounts of relational or extended abstract thinking.

Issue 5: Reluctance in Sharing of Practice

As a small discipline, this community should be sharing practice to learn from each other and build on each other's successes and failures (Lave & Wenger, 1991). But due to its lack of critical mass in the educational sector, the programmes are vulnerable to small changes in the market forces which mean that programme leaders are often reluctant to share information on their pedagogical approaches as it may affect their competitive edge. However, if the search for appropriate pedagogy can only be socially constructed by knowing what has been done before and how it can be improved on, the isolation of these pedagogical approaches may cause the discipline to be slow to change with respect to other disciplines. Therefore the sharing of pedagogical knowledge by the community of medical physicists' academics needs to be more altruistic if the medical physics pedagogy is expected to be developed further. Alternatively, these academics can join communities of practice that are closely related to their discipline in which they can build their appropriate pedagogy.

Issue 6: Nepotism in the Discipline

The Medical Physics discipline may suffer from nepotism in which a few experienced persons may determine its pedagogical direction in a dictatorial approach. However, it is important that junior academics and other stakeholders are given a voice to contribute to its search for an appropriate pedagogy as they may have fresh ideas and the energy to implement and test new ideas that are appropriate for the discipline. A junior academic presence on accreditation panel activities, guided by experienced professionals, may offer a means to reduce nepotism by blending the fresh insights of educationally-trained junior academics with the opinions of experienced and established members.

Issue 7: Changes by External Bodies

The issue of changes of accreditation standards by external bodies is likely linked to Issue 6. The direction of the discipline is inevitably determined by these external bodies as they decide what the characteristics of the Medical Physics graduate are and hence to some extent dictate what the degree programmes should look like. To ensure that these changes are not unexpected and continue to ensure the adaptation of an appropriate pedagogy, it is essential that programme leaders are in dialogue with the external bodies and provide comments on consultations about the pedagogical direction of the discipline. In turn, the guest lecturers and junior academic staff need to be in a two-way dialogue with the educational leaders on professional body education or accreditation panels to share their ideas and concerns, and to allow staff members to adapt as early as possible to changes.

Issue 8: Meeting the Needs of the Students

This is perhaps the most important challenge as the search for an appropriate pedagogy should be about ensuring that the needs of the students are being met. It is perhaps difficult to know what these needs may be as this may be range from developing their Medical Physics identity, helping them to follow a particular employability path and meeting the needs of the job market. If the student needs are placed at the heart of the search for the appropriate pedagogy, then there is a better likelihood of these being met. However, the discipline needs to determine clearly what these important requirements are by listening to their students, external bodies and the employment market and then acting upon these drivers. It is possible that in dealing with Issues 1–7, that Issue 8 will follow, particularly in respect to governmental changes, such as the TEF in the UK, at least, are designed to encourage more appropriate pedagogies. The TEF is envisioned by policy makers, will better promote independent learning within a supported environment so that teaching quality is raised across the sector, particularly with respect to metrics such as student satisfaction, graduate employment rates, proportions of graduates in highly skilled jobs and completion rates on programmes.

FINAL THOUGHTS

In a higher education landscape where greater scrutiny is being applied to educational performance metrics for undergraduate and postgraduate education, small sub-disciplines may be vulnerable to being closed or merged with other disciplines due to their small offerings, the possible number of students and the number of qualified teachers. The search for an appropriate pedagogy may continue and evolve as small disciplines try and determine their identity based on what type of knowledge field they wish to inhabit (soft/hard; pure/applied). To aid in this search, there needs to be some disciplinary professional or external body which can guide its development in a cohesive manner which meets the interests of the discipline, students and the employability market.

REFERENCES

Biggs, J. (1996). Enhancing teaching through constructive alignment. *Higher Education, 32*(3), 347–364.
Biggs, J. (1999). What the student does: Teaching for enhanced learning. *Higher Education Research & Development, 18*(1), 57–75.
Biggs, J., & Tang, C. (2007). *Teaching for quality learning at university* (3rd ed.). Buckingham: The Open University Press.
Biglan, A. (1973a). The characteristics of subject matter in different academic areas. *Journal of Applied Psychology, 57*(3), 195–203.
Biglan, A. (1973b). Relationships between subject matter characteristics and the structure and output of university departments. *Journal of Applied Psychology, 57*(3), 204–213.
Bloom, B. S. (1956). *Taxonomy of educational objectives, handbook I: The cognitive domain*. New York, NY: David McKay Co., Inc.
Crawford, K., Gordon, S., Nicholas, J., & Prosser, M. (1998). University mathematics students' conceptions of mathematics. *Studies in Higher Education, 23*(1), 87–94.
Diamond, A., Vorley, T., Roberts, J., & Jones, S. (2012). *Behavioural approaches to understanding student choice*. York: The Higher Education Academy.
Dinkins, C. S. (2005). Shared inquiry: Socratic-hermeneutic interpre-viewing. In P. M. Ironside (Ed.), *Beyond method: Philosophical conversations in healthcare research and scholarship* (pp. 111–147). Madison, WI: University of Wisconsin Press.
Drake, B., Hovmand, P., Jonson-Reid, M., & Zayas, L. H. (2007). Adopting and teaching evidence-based practice in master's-level social work programs. *Journal of Social Work Education, 43*(3), 431–446.
Entwistle, N., & Tait, H. (1990). Approaches to learning, evaluations of teaching and preferences for contrasting academic environments. *Higher Education, 19*(2), 169–194.
Gow, L., & Kember, D. (1990). Does higher education promote independent learning? *Higher Education, 19*(3), 307–322.

Hinchliffe, G. W., & Jolly, A. (2011). Graduate identity and employability. *British Educational Research Journal, 37*(4), 563–584.

Hosein, A. (2005). *Teaching of linear programming: Variation across disciplines and countries* (Unpublished MSc dissertation). Open University, Milton Keynes.

Huang, R. (2005). Chinese international students' perceptions of the problem-based learning experience. *Journal of Hospitality, Leisure, Sport and Tourism Education, 4*(2), 36–43.

Krathwohl, D. R. (2002). A revision of Bloom's taxonomy: An overview. *Theory Into Practice, 41*(4), 212–218.

Lave, J., & Wenger, E. (1991). *Situated learning: Legitimate peripheral participation.* Cambridge: Cambridge University Press.

Marton, F., & Säljö, R. (1976). On qualitative differences in learning: I-outcome and process. *British Journal of Educational Psychology, 46*(1), 4–11.

Vu, H., & Doyle, S. (2014). Across borders and across cultures: Vietnamese students' positioning of teachers in a university twinning programme. *Journal of Education for Teaching, 40*(3), 267–283.

Wakeham, W. (2016). *Wakeham review of STEM degree provision and graduate employability.* London: Department for Business, Innovation & Skills and Higher Education Funding Council for England.

Watkins, D., Dahlin, B., & Ekholm, M. (2005). Awareness of the backwash effect of assessment: A phenomenographic study of the views of Hong Kong and Swedish lecturers. *Instructional Science, 33*(4), 283–309.

Anesa Hosein
Department of Higher Education
University of Surrey
Guildford, UK

Jamie Harle
Department of Medical Physics & Biomedical Engineering
University College London
London, UK

RICHARD WATERMEYER AND MICHAEL TOMLINSON

6. THE MARKETIZATION OF PEDAGOGY AND THE PROBLEM OF 'COMPETITIVE ACCOUNTABILITY'

INTRODUCTION

From a neoliberal purview, competition is a vital and virtuous aspect of capitalism that mobilizes economic activity, trade and markets. Through the financial pay-offs it helps to accrue, competition can incentivize the '*performance*' of those we might broadly define as '*economic actors*', and feed their ambitions and aspirations to become more competitive and thus more profitable participants or '*producers*' within a market economy system. Competition is accordingly rationalized as a *good thing*, where producers commit themselves to '*out-performing*' their competitors by creating more competitive products – and ostensibly, by extension greater product choice – that benefit the consumer but which also generate for the producer, profit, market position and/or dominance and power. Accordingly competition can be what encourages producers to be more innovative, imaginative, creative, experimental, reflexive, daring and risk-taking as they seek out what is an habitually elusive prize of originality, which will set them apart, make them distinct, and consequently afford them advantage over their market competitors. Competition is, therefore, in the simplest of terms, the pathway to economic success; the successful negotiation of which may culminate in claims of being the best.

Competition or the degree to which economic actors are competitive would thus seem to dictate the extent of economic health and prosperity at the meso (the institution or organization) and macro (the nation-state) level. In the latter category, the contemporary, dominant political theorization of national success is one that connects market competitiveness with economic strength. Unsurprisingly, therefore, the industrialized nations of the world have for so long had the edge, competitively and have therefore dominated the global economic and therefore political landscape. The status quo is, however, now changing with the challenge presented by the BRIC economies especially, whose embrace of the '*free*' market, has engendered in part, accelerated change and huge strides in the degree to which they now operate as competitive producers within a global market economy; much perhaps to the alarm and loosening grip of the old economic order of industrialized nations (cf. Altbach, 2016).

The word '*global*' here is integral, as is the qualification of economic markets being '*free*' – a qualification we shall contest herein – to a discussion of the way with which economic actors now position themselves as producers that operate increasingly in markets without borders, where competition has massively enlarged and where a requirement for competitiveness is absolute. But what of all this to education and specifically educational providers? What is the implication of competition and *global* competition at that? To understand the significance of competition to the field of education, and as is germane to our discussion, higher education specifically, observers need not look far before being forcefully confronted with the spectacle of the impact of an ethos of market competitiveness on the university and its inhabitants.

THE UNIVERSITY IN CRISIS: A CONCEPT OF 'COMPETITIVE ACCOUNTABILITY'

As has been well documented by many researchers working in the field of higher education studies and education studies more broadly, the university as it advances towards the end of the second decade of the new millennium, is an institution and ideology best described as in a state of flux and transition (cf. Collini, 2012; Deem, Hillyard, & Reed, 2007; Giroux, 2014). While for some this kind of characterization is nothing new and indeed is something of the hallmark of the university's character, much as it could be said to be of science, the extent of such volatility and change, particularly in response to global forces is felt by many within its community to be especially acute (cf. King, Marginson, & Naidoo, 2011). Many scholars have observed the effects of globalization on higher education and moreover how globalization has caused the intensification and for most neoliberal acolytes the necessity of market logic in the rationalization and organization of higher education. An ability to evidence and mobilize market worth – where market worth is taken as shorthand for the contribution to national economic health; frequently (mis)assumed to be and conflated with, social wellbeing – has become even more of an issue in the context of the aftermath of the events of 2008 and global economic downturn. The ramifications of global recession have arguably been felt most painfully by the public sector and therefore publically funded services and institutions, of which of course in the United Kingdom (UK), much like most other countries, higher education is one.

As two academics working within the UK higher education system we have experienced at first hand, how both a downturn in global and national economic fortunes yet also importantly a politics of austerity initiated by a Tory and Liberal Democrat coalition government, in the distribution of public funds has placed huge pressure on universities to demonstrate their value. More specifically, universities in the UK have found themselves increasingly compelled to respond and stand up to public scrutiny where they are receivers of significant investment from the public purse. Part of the intensifying spotlight on what academics do is also related to an idea of the university as detached, disinterested and dislocated from the public sphere. This is a sentiment that this has contributed to public suspicion and mistrust of scientists, which might only be corrected with the dismantling of the idea and practice of the university as an ivory-tower and the forging of a more porous interface involving science and society (Watermeyer, 2011). Consequently, as one aspect of the university's portfolio, research conducted across the UK's higher education system, funded by the public purse has come under even greater scrutiny. Public funding for research in UK universities is administered via a dual support system: open response mode funding distributed by disciplinary specific research councils and quality related research (QR) monies made available to universities on the basis of their performance within a national evaluation exercise, known as the Research Excellence Framework.

While it is not necessary to discuss in any depth the consequences of these two conduits for research funding on research praxis and practitioners, it would be remiss of us not to consider how enhanced scrutiny of the research funding landscape, reflects, indeed reinforces the challenges met by academics' other role as teachers. Crucially, what can be gleaned from changes in research funding for academics in UK universities is the greater focus on what we might call '*competitive accountability*'. This we take as the extent to which academics, in this instance in the context of research funding – the award for which occurs traditionally via a process of peer-evaluation, which has involved more recently in the terms of the REF, the value judgments of user-assessors – have their research identities, practice and priorities influenced and albeit indirectly governed by a competitive process, where they are forced to sell themselves as producers of public benefits or in other words, the public good. The way this is achieved is twofold. In the context of funding provided by the UK's research councils, applicants are required to detail what they anticipate to be the prospective impact of their research and how they plan to achieve this. In the context of the REF, successor to the Research Assessment Exercise (RAE), in to which a requirement for articulating and evidencing the economic and societal impact of research was formalized for the first time (and as a twenty percent component of the overall exercise), university researchers were asked to produce narrative case studies that offered an historical record of their impact achievements. In both cases academics' impact would be determined by disciplinary experts and user-assessors, whose judgments would form the basis of funding decisions.

An impact era for higher education in the UK has been contested for the ways with which it confuses public accountability with auditability and has caused a divergence away from academics committing to and fulfilling a moral obligation of the public good substituted with their committing to and fulfilling a fiscal obligation of securing their institutions' '*positional goods*'. Furthermore, in so doing they are responsible for the perpetuation of positional markets and wider inter-institutional competition.

It is concurrently criticized for causing academics to capitulate to what Mats Alveson (2013) has called '*the triumph of emptiness*' and a sense of prioritizing what Chubb and Watermeyer (2016) have described as 'artifice over integrity'. The emergence of '*competitive accountability*' among academics may be attributed to what some see as the '*spectre*' of performance management, the privileging and/

or emergence of a cult of administration or administrators as bearers of a kind of managerial fundamentalism and intolerant enforcers of a culture of audit, surveillance and compliance, that culminates in academics – fearful for their very livelihoods – to fall in line. Academics '*selling themselves*' as impact-merchants may be further attributed to reconciling a demand that they embody '*excellence*' – an infinitely amorphous and non-consensual qualification – with the parsimony associated with the distribution of public funds for research and an overall science budget, coupled with the agnosticism[1] of the policy community in terms of what it recognizes as the societal value and contribution of academic research and expertise. Moreover, we fear that academics' corroboration with '*competitive accountability*' has become normalized and latent; a perhaps unnoticed and unconsciously enacted aspect of academic labour nonetheless ingrained and ubiquitous within the very fabric of the neoliberal university and arguably, to our minds at least, helped along by academics', if not universal, lapse into hubris. This is not to say there is only wholesale deference. There do exist pockets of resistance or evidence of counter-hegemonic discourse and activism, though these we argue tend to occur furtively in subterranean – or frequently digital – domains.

What we thus see and experience in the contemporary economic and political configuration of the university is what some commentators like Michael Burawoy (2011) describe as a crisis, and others particularly critical pedagogues like Henry Giroux denounce as neoliberalism's war on higher education. We ourselves have reflected on the way with which what Naidoo (2016) calls '*a competition fetish*' has destabilized our sense of identity and mission as academics, which is at the best of times fragile, and has in ways that are conspicuously antithetical to traditional Mertonian and Enlightenment notions of scholarship, caused to enervate academics' ties with a project of critical democracy. Indeed, we suggest that the reality of the situation academics face is one where who they are and what they do becomes corrupted on the basis of their forced compliance and collusion with a system of '*competitive accountability*'.

But '*competitive accountability*' is not just a phenomena or means of characterizing academia that is exclusive to research domains; though most recently this has tended to be where the '*public*' gaze has fixed – magnified by changes to research evaluation and funding. The marketization and massification of higher education, including the internationalization of universities, are forces of huge change for what it means to teach and be a teacher in a higher education context, with multiple parallels to research in what may be perceived as a deteriorating contract.

THE NEOLIBERALIZATION OF TEACHING IN HIGHER EDUCATION

The introduction in England of tuition fees following the recommendations of the Dearing report in 1998 and the uncapping of student numbers more recently in 2015 are two events that symbolize the total transition of the English university into a mass market economy of higher education.[2] In the current context where undergraduate tuition fees stand and stand to rise above a threshold of nine thousand pounds per annum, it is not only the university who is said to have changed as it adjusts to its role as a competitive market provider. The economization of higher education has to many minds fundamentally altered the nature of the university's relationship with its students, and accordingly the way that students conceive of themselves.

Many academics – including ourselves – teaching in English higher education have detected an attitudinal shift among the student population and an accompanying change or rather elevation in terms of their expectations of the university experience and the benefits to be accrued from it. Accordingly, the identity of the undergraduate student has morphed from knowledge apprentice to credential consumer, whose university participation is predominantly justified as a down-payment on their attaining enhanced competitiveness within a global graduate labour market. Yet when, in recent times of global economic frailty, the surety of enhanced transition provided by post-compulsory education to employment has faltered and with it confidence and belief in the university as a catalyst of social mobility, a cost-benefit analysis for what may be regarded as high-premium participation becomes all the more prevalent.

Students are frequently portrayed as savvy consumers of a higher education product, whose understanding of what universities offer and what specific institutions provide is more accomplished and comprehensive than that of previous generations for whom higher education was without entrance tax and without need for market analysis. Universities consequently, have had to substantially raise their game in enticing students to enrol on their programmes. Their marketing departments are nevermore so central to the way they position and advertise themselves to an external audience whose recruitment is indispensable to their survival and future as educational providers and competitive market players. Concurrently, academic staff are called upon to act as peddlers flogging their curricular wares to prospective students and their parents in what feel like an endless and uninterrupted cycle of open days and marketing events. These, for many academics, are occasions of reticent entrepreneurialism, discomfort and distaste at feeling forced into perpetuating a horribly reductionist discourse of higher education as nothing more than a consumerist product. Moreover, for some is a sense of disingenuousness where their coerced complicity in selling a utopian dream of higher education belies the uncertain and insecure reality so many undergraduates face upon completion of their studies and a backdrop for many, of the handicap of significant debt accrued.

Nonetheless, universities fly the flag that boasts of their multiple resources and achievements; the quality of their student accommodation; the extensiveness of their sports and recreational facilities; their links with business and industry and their placement schemes; and perhaps increasingly most tellingly, their status as educational providers as conferred by their ranking in national and international league tables. In this latter context especially, what students associate as the best higher education providers, beyond the archetypes of Cambridge and Oxford, are associations informed by benchmarks of quality calculated for instance through student satisfaction surveys, that measure in rather contrived yet high-currency ways, the '*quality*' of educational provision. Consequently, universities that score highly in evaluation exercises like the UK's National Student Survey are ostensibly one-step ahead of their competitors in attracting high numbers of the best students. And while maintaining pole-position in '*quality*' related league tables is for most institutions difficult if not impossible, an institutional focus and investment in strong performance is a constant if not intensifying aspect of the performance management of academic teachers.

Whilst satisfaction surveys of the kind described can in ways be beneficial both as an outlet for the student voice and as a means of gaining insight into the student mindset, the extent to which they provide an accurate and reliable reading of pedagogical quality is very much open to debate; not least where judgments of pedagogical quality are based upon the dis/satisfaction of the student as a consumer. How then do we begin to evaluate and attribute quality to pedagogy in higher education and is this even possible and/or worthwhile? Furthermore, might evaluation of this sort produce adverse consequences both for teachers and their students? Are we as educators slouching towards a sense of '*critical pedagogy in dark times*' as Henry Giroux (2011) puts it, and the eschewal of good quality teaching and learning as that which is disruptive and challenging for the privileging of learning as a process of instant gratification? Analogously, is not one of the more perverse outcomes of student-consumerism the production of learners who are ill-suited to the modern labour market?

In the current UK context a government policy for evaluation for teaching has hardened and formalized within what is rather opaquely understood as the REF's teaching-focused cousin, the Teaching Excellence Framework (TEF). The TEF is opaque in the minds of most academics simply because most of its effects are yet to be felt as it remains essentially in a phase of formative development, but also, crucially, because many academics as teachers and pedagogical experts, dismiss the efficacy of a standardized system that tests teaching proficiency in universities where there is such huge pedagogical diversity and variance and which is then used to justify fee-enhancements. We agree. But did we not mention that the TEF is interpreted as another feeder of league tables and method for justifying the fees institutions charge? So yet again, an interest and focus on the quality of teaching in universities is fundamentally underpinned not by pedagogical but commercial motivation. It seems less about how academics can more effectively reflect, learn from and improve their teaching and more about how academics can perform more successfully in evaluation '*competitions*'; because that essentially is what a performance culture in higher education and what we have thus referred to as '*competitive accountability*' produces.

What we perceive as the explicit danger of '*competitive accountability*' is the bizarre obfuscation and potential false-claiming of excellence as it might describe either teaching or research. We compare this situation to what teachers, educational researchers and employers lament of systems of rote learning and/or teaching to the test that are so ingrained in the psyche of schools and their assessment systems yet which nurture little more than technical proficiency and an ability to respond to basic performance-evaluation conditions. Yet what of skills of lateral or critical thinking? Forsaken we must presume for the greater surety attributed to higher level percentage pass rates, that characterize a school's performance, in competitive performance league tables. Higher education similarly seems to have fallen foul of a similar fate and appears intent on valorizing academics who perform successfully in the context of league table qualifications of success that may have no correlation to a sense of excellence – we repeat our assertion, as an empty qualifier – that occurs in the classroom.

The fetishization of competition and more specifically league tables by universities represents, we would suggest, the kowtowing of educators to commercial demands and moreover an abnegation of duty to their students. The fundamental problem with the kinds of direct (and more indirect in the case of teaching) performance related funding established in the REF and TEF, is the danger it poses for academics to lose their professional bearings and a more authentic and intuitive sense of what matters and what's important in teaching and research, which will likely have nothing to do with crude and potentially arbitrary evaluative scores. Ultimately, universities and academics run the risk of focusing so much on their market appeal through evaluative rankings that they may lose sight of the fundamentals of research and teaching. Furthermore, there is a serious danger that the consumer paradigm of higher education, massively underestimates its student base and the potential of the pedagogical interface, the fulfilment of which requires reciprocal exchange and knowledge co-production.

THE CONSTRICTION OF THE PEDAGOGICAL IMAGINATION AND FORECLOSING OF CRITICALITY

A major issue for academic teachers working in higher education's '*audit society*' (cf. Strathern, 2000; Shore & Wright, 1999), is the extent to which their obligation to dance to the tune of performance measures disincentivizes and suffocates their creative intelligence, expression and freedom as classroom practitioners. Many of our colleagues and those we have worked with, sometimes in a mentoring capacity, with less experience or knowledge of pedagogy, articulate a sense of fear and trepidation in exceeding the bounds of what their students expect of them and, therefore, doing anything that might compromise their performance (and scores) within module and programme student evaluations. For some this translates into a straitjacket experience where they feel compelled to play it safe in the classroom and in their interactions with students; to stick with tried and tested formula; and do anything to protect upsetting the performance-evaluation apple cart. The great irony, as it appears, therefore, is that performance evaluation far from providing a stimulus for ameliorated classroom practice – which, we relate to pedagogical innovativeness, creativity and a capacity to transcend the basic function of teaching as the transmission of knowledge – may actually cause teachers to '*reign-in*' and adopt a more conservative, bland, uninspiring and purely functional pedagogical philosophy and approach. In such terms, the creative and critical agency of academics as teachers and perhaps most significantly, their capacity and confidence in challenging their students in ways that might facilitate, broaden and enrich their acquisition of knowledge and skills, is threatened.

A motif of '*the consumer knows best*' and what the consumer wants the producer must provide is especially troublesome in the context of pedagogical development or rather its regression. Such a motif fails to recognize and is perhaps even a rejection of what we perceive as both the science and artistry of pedagogy and the pedagogue therefore as someone with albeit, varying levels of mastery and expertise. Where university teaching becomes, as many already believe it has, consumer led, then the authority of the academic as teacher and master of her/his subject is entirely compromised as is also we propose, the sustainability of the teacher/student interface as one of expert and apprentice. Our argument is not, however, one that seeks to dismiss the value of a democratically organized and student-invested form of higher education, rather that the achievement of this can only occur where the academic as teacher is given license to operate with autonomy and with trust in her/his ability. Fundamentally, we would argue, a system of continuous performance evaluation signifies the ultimate betrayal of trust in academics and teachers and an overall sense perhaps that they are just not up to the job.

Higher education has regrettably suffered historically from an opinion that academics are frequently far from the best teachers. For most graduates of higher education, the experience of an endlessly uninspiring, perhaps mind numbingly boring lecture/r are never too far from memory. Academics have of course never tended to experience nor required the same kinds of professional training as have school-teachers and have accrued their expertise of the classroom on the job. Consequently, it's fair to say there has been broad variation in terms of the investment made by academics in honing their craft as teachers and the extent to which this has translated into effective classroom practice. Teaching in higher education, furthermore, has tended to suffer from lower status, particularly when compared to research, which to this day in UK universities remains the highest mark of esteem. Many academics, and in truth we reflect ourselves at least partially within this, engage in research funding activity not only so that they might undertake research – and of course in fulfillment of their contractual obligations where income generation through competitive research funds is a standard expectation – but so that they can '*buy*' themselves out of teaching. In other words, teaching for many academics is something they would frankly rather not do and is encumbrance upon their preferred pursuit of research. Given these multiple contexts, universities and higher education regulators (and quality assurance providers) and support organizations have placed increased focus on the professionalization of academics as teachers; which in many ways seems only fair where the income generated from teaching is significant and indispensable to the running of institutions. Consequently, universities in the UK are awash with training for academics, particularly for those at earlier stages of an academic career or with less classroom experience, which in many instances forms a mandatory part of their probation. Furthermore, academics are encouraged to seek professional accreditation as teachers through the form of, for instance, fellowship of the UK's Higher Education Academy. In other words, academics as teachers in UK universities are, in response to an historical deficit and bias but also forms of market quality control – which we understand to encompass the external accreditation of academic taught-programmes; student evaluation; and the kinds of teaching peer-review envisaged in the TEF – becoming more credentialed as teachers. Our question and concern, however, remains: to what extent does such a focus on market-led quality control produce the conditions from which teachers can flourish as pedagogues and where students can most benefit?

In the specific context of what counts in higher education curricula, a sense that academics know best, even where the curriculum they design may be research led, is increasingly contested. This is especially the case, where we observe paradigm shifts related to knowledge production and the overall role of the university in relation to the public sphere. At the meso (institutional) level we perceive '*competitive accountability*' occurring at the level of a triple-helix interface of universities working synergistically, though frequently as a more junior partner, with government and industry/business. At a macro level we observe migration from a more traditional model of knowledge production that privileges self-sovereign scholastic inquiry to a Mode-2 version of knowledge co-production that unites academics with research stakeholders and users. A greater focusing of curriculum design and development as it meets the needs and core requirements of industry as graduate employers also seems to wrest the responsibility of what is taught, and therefore we can confidently suppose how it is taught from academics. An enhanced focus on university-industry alignment, particularly in the context of curriculum, also suggests the increasing utilitarianisation of higher education and a value of higher education more or less exclusively understood in terms of employability. Moreover we suggest that the turning of higher education into a commercial transaction and culture of student consumerism has deleterious pedagogical implications manifest for instance in surface learning; the valorization of edutainment; an erosion of trust between students and teachers; and the normalization and proliferation of a culture of litigation.

These are all aspects of the changing ontological and epistemological contours of higher education that are redefining and also causing significant limitations paradoxically to teaching in universities and what we propose as the potential hollowing-out and homogenization of pedagogy, which seems also to reflect wider trends of institutional isomorphism engendered by (global) marketization. The homogenization of pedagogy in higher education is especially problematic and antagonistic to our sensibility first of the university as a rich tapestry of different kinds of pedagogical experiences, but also of a notion of academics engaged within a project of criticality and as enablers of the critical agency and citizenship of their students. Indeed, we perceive a dichotomy between a notion of pedagogy,

95

particularly a critical pedagogy of the likes pursued by theorists and activists like Paolo Freire, bell hooks and Henry Giroux, and the professionalization of teaching that now dominates.

With the ascent of professionalization in university teaching we perceive a cognate domestication of pedagogy and the disempowerment of both faculty and students to engage with education as a political project and one, which exceeds the functional determinism privileged by educational and occupational markets and academic capitalists. A crass but nonetheless powerful meme that supports such a view is that of the student *buying* their 2:1 degree as if their '*higher*' education is nothing bar a process to acquiring advanced rights of labour market participation. Indeed, we might even reflect that higher education in the market realm is rationalized first and foremost as a commercial transaction. And accordingly given to the high economic stakes of the student as an investor in her/his occupational future and the academic teacher as a procurer of finance and prestige to her/his institution, the dominance of a transactional model deepens and all seemingly fall into line.

The corralling of criticality and the emergence of conformist pedagogy is made again horribly lucid and tangible through what can be observed across the world as the turning of university campuses into '*safe spaces*' (cf. Furedi, 2004; Slater, 2016; Williams, 2016). We have now in higher education new taxonomies such as '*trigger warnings*', that are used to account for forms of behaviour and types of discourse among faculty and students that are perceived to be transgressive and at odds with a neoliberal status-quo; words, thoughts and deeds that might contaminate and risk the sterility of an apolitical and non-critical safe space. Disagreement, contestation, argumentation are seemingly abandoned and quarantined in a new nanny state of nodding heads. Best not to question less the question leads you to difficult and unresolvable answers. The very rubric of science appears under threat. But as recent, and not so recent political events have demonstrated, science and the work of scientists appears of scant value in the formation of public policy, whether that be in the context of political and economic union or in the context of climate change. The right for free speech on campus similarly appears to close, where those with values other than the consensus are condemned as maleficent. Freedom for self-expression whether that be in the context of a student's contribution to a tutorial discussion or the kinds of ideas brought up by an academic within a lecture is similarly also threatened. The crisis of the university is thus it would seem the culmination of multiple aspects driven ultimately by market diktat and what we have identified as '*competitive accountability*' and the reduction of education into a project that has resulted in the sanitization of ideas; the turning of criticality in contraband; and the infantilization of faculty and students.

CONCLUSION

We return to a point made in the earlier parts of this chapter, which referred to the underestimation of students by those who enforce and police – with zero-tolerance we might add – a neoliberal mandate and an assumption that the evisceration of pedagogy by market forces correlates to the collapse of the student as a critical agent. Whilst, we cannot help but think and see the effect of a consumer model of higher education in terms of how it prescribes student identity, we also observe a different kind of effect fomented by the imposition of such a framing.

Exercises in critical activism perpetuated by students that have occurred within and out with university campuses across the world in the course of the last few years demonstrate both the efficacy of an alternative imagining of pedagogy and the plausibility of critical pedagogy at that. We have witnessed in higher education through various forms of student protest, sit-ins and occupations and coordinated digitally mediated campaigns, active resistance and rebellion against the neoliberalization of the university and its capitulation to market logic. Protest from within the UK, across Europe, the United States and South Africa have evidenced the coalescing of students in critical solidarity against the commercialization of seemingly every facet of higher education, the kinds of unequal participation this brings, and moreover the way their identities have been reduced to '*paying customers*'. Whilst their protest may in no way signify or typify the views of the majority, their dissent is a break and challenge to the normative depiction of the passive consumer. The picture is self-evidently more complex and more nuanced. Furthermore, this kind of dissonance is richly symbolic of a different kind of accountability, the university's own to itself as democratic institution, especially where reports of institutional handling of student activism reveal the reverse and signs of despotic rule.

At the same time as students display coordinated leadership in a demand for institutional (less academic) accountability, the precariousness of academic labour and the lack of feasible '*exit-strategies*' for many, means that a majority of academics are less conspicuous, indeed even intentionally covert in their attempts at reclaiming an explicitly '*critical*' pedagogy. We do, however, see evidence of a growing polemic and signs of better organization by academics in attempting a reconversion of the classroom and one that situates a form of accountability which is other than '*competitive*'. We ourselves are activists involved in defending against the evisceration of pedagogy and the subjugation and infantilization of students by commercial values. We seek to free pedagogy from its coupling with performance.

Our efforts surely as those of most academics must be not as custodians of a safe-space but as consorts or chaperones that guide our students and help to guide themselves through the rocky and often dangerous terrain of knowledge. We must embrace the danger and risk of science and the risk of exposure through pedagogy in respect and fulfillment of the university and its mission as a space of '*higher*' learning. We ought to protect against the disillusionment, inertia and impasse brought by conformity by listening to the critical demands, even if they be only whimpers of our students. Our accountability as academics might then transform as Samuel Bowles argues from a commercial and thus '*competitive*' to a moral imperative.

NOTES

[1] An agnosticism that seems more firmly entrenched and even surpassed in the context of a post-Brexit UK and a rejection of the contribution of expertise to public policy.
[2] In the other UK nations, higher education remains free for Scottish nationals and in Wales access to higher education has been up until recently heavily subsidized by the devolved Assembly Government.

REFERENCES

Altbach, P. G. (2016). *Global perspectives on higher education*. Baltimore, MD: Johns Hopkins University Press.

Alveson, M. (2013). *The triumph of emptiness: Consumption, higher education and work organization*. Oxford: Oxford University Press.

Burawoy, M. (2011). Redefining the public university: Global and national contexts. In J. Holmwood (Ed.), *A manifesto for the public university* (pp. 27–41). London: Bloomsbury Academic.

Chubb, J., & Watermeyer, R. (2016). Artifice or integrity in the marketization of research impact? Investigating the moral economy of (pathways to) impact statements within research funding proposals in the UK and Australia. *Studies in Higher Education, 42*(12), 2360–2372. doi:10.1080/03075079.2016.1144182

Collini, S. (2012). *What are universities for?* London: Penguin Books.

Deem, R., Hillyard, S., & Reed, M. (2007). *Knowledge, higher education and the new managerialism*. Oxford: Oxford University Press.

Furedi, F. (2004). *Where have all the intellectuals gone? Confronting 21st century philisitinism*. London & New York, NY: Continuum.

Giroux, H. (2011). *On critical pedagogy*. London: Bloomsbury Academic.

Giroux, H. (2014). *Neoliberalism's war on higher education*. Chicago, IL: Haymarket Books.

King, R., Marginson, S., & Naidoo, R. (Eds.). (2011). *Handbook on globalization and higher education*. Cheltenham: Edward Elgar.

Naidoo, R. (2016). The competition fetish in higher education: Varieties, animators and consequences. *British Journal of Sociology of Education, 37*(1), 1–10.

Slater, T. (Ed.). (2016). *Unsafe space: The crisis of free speech on campus*. Basingstoke: Palgrave Macmillan.

Shore, C., & Wright, S. (1999). Audit culture and anthropology: Neoliberalism in British higher education. *The Journal of the Royal Anthropological Institute, 5*(4), 557–575.

Strathern, M. (2000). *Audit cultures: Anthropological studies in accountability, ethics and the academy*. London: Routledge.

The Dearing Report. (1997). *Higher education in the learning society*. London: HMSO.

Watermeyer, R. (2011). Challenges for engagement: Toward a public academe? *Higher Education Quarterly, 65*(4), 386–410.

Williams, J. (2016). *Academic freedom in an age of conformity: Confronting the fear of knowledge*. Basingstoke: Palgrave Macmillan.

Richard Watermeyer
Department of Education
University of Bath
Bath, UK

Michael Tomlinson
Southampton Education School
University of Southampton
Southampton, UK

GILL NICHOLLS AND SIMON LYGO-BAKER

7. STRATEGIC PEDAGOGIC MANAGEMENT

*Balancing Act or Symbiotic Relationship between
Enhancement and Assurance*

INTRODUCTION

This chapter explores the architecture of the higher education landscape through the experience of Gill, a senior manager, via a conversation with Simon, a colleague she has worked with for a number of years. This is framed by exploring her own journey and how this has shaped and been shaped by the different structures, policies and people encountered. The chapter explores the experiences drawn from a range of organisations framed against a disciplinary background that involved working in the UK and the USA. This approach allows the illumination and exploration of a series of tensions between pedagogical experimentation and the resistance to change set against a fast adapting set of frameworks.

The conversation was based around an informal conversational approach (Gall et al., 2003) which allowed for different aspects to be picked upon as they arose, although some structure was provided by following a general chronological approach to Gill's career path. It was believed that such an approach would enable the most natural response. Gill and Simon have worked together for many years and therefore have experienced many conversations which have explored learning and teaching approaches in a range of different UK institutions. It was therefore felt that using an informal conversation approach would closely mirror these experiences and was more likely to illicit insights that a more structured interview may limit (Turner, 2010). The approach taken therefore provided Simon with flexibility to respond to the comments made and allow the flow to remain, using Gill's career timeline as a general guide when needed to move the conversation forward. The conversation started by asking Gill to consider a broad question at the outset of how she saw the relationship between enhancement and assurance. The conversation then traced her experiences as a learner before turning to reflect upon her role as a teacher. This explored her different roles as a student, then as a researcher and teacher within science before moving into education and finally more senior positions including advising more strategic approaches at a national level.

ENHANCEMENT AND ASSURANCE

The conversation started by exploring how enhancement is used to frame current strategic actions. Gill reflected that the framing of enhancement has moved to ensuring that students appear at the very least to be '*happy*'. From a senior management position this can be a strategic activity because it is more likely that if current students reflect happiness within the institution that this is more likely to encourage a steady stream of future students. Gill felt that this is where the debates between enhancement and assurance appear to have moved us currently. However, she noted it may not need to be perceived in this way. Rather with a subtle shift it could be conceived of as being considered as what is the best opportunity that a student can have in the learning environment that is set and how can an institution manage these opportunities within legislative constructs. That is extremely challenging because ultimately every student is an individual and you clearly cannot adapt to each of those individual approaches. You therefore have to look towards developing consensus through dialogue with the learners. At the same time it is important to consider the infrastructure that will allow the learners to receive a consistent learning environment that can also be managed and sustained by the institution.

Asked how you begin such a process Gill argued that you need to put the student at the centre. Doing so allows you to examine what it is that we do to them as learners and what it is that they do to us and where can, and do, these actions meet. The danger is that if we do not examine the reality of this we continue to potentially develop practice that does not engage the students and produces gaps. These gaps can lead ultimately to less satisfied students. This is where Gill suggested the enhancement comes in when we start to recognise that we are moving the learners from a position where they are not engaged with material to a situation where they are. If you can then increase the engagement and time the students engage with the material (Berliner, 1984) the likely result is that you ultimately gain higher quality outcomes. If we do this, then that lessens the need to be seen to focus on notions of quality from a bureaucratic perspective that is characterised by a tick-box, process driven approach. Although it may sound idealistic, such an approach if understood by a senior management team can enable the student to be seen to guide the strategy of the institution from both strands – enhancement and assurance.

Gill went on that in exploring the complex dynamics that can exist between enhancement and assurance it is important to consider both the financial context of your portfolio which includes staff, estates and resources and the legislative side. Sometimes these two areas may appear to be in conflict. However, she suggested that there are times when the legislative interpretation is used as a way to restrict enhancement and that can create a significant challenge that removes the centrality of the student. As a senior manager there needs to be careful consideration of what people and teams are needed to enable the quality that leads to the student gaining enhancement.

Within this landscape there are a significant number of voices competing to be heard. The predominant ones are often related to the status quo and there is a danger that these voices will put challenges in the way (Lane, 2007) even if they offer limited or no alternative (Stephenson & Yorke, 1998). This can also apply to the student, who may put up challenges because it is not want they want. Gill acknowledged that the authority of the student voice had undoubtedly appeared to grow with the instigation of fees (Bates & Kaye, 2014). Gill acknowledged that this is important but that for her the student should be the most central and it should not be influenced by the aspect of fees. Gill noted she would not want to call them a customer indicating that this can be a distraction from the important dialogue that needs to occur. Reflecting on her experience at different institutions she added that the relationship that the student has with each institution can differ depending on the mission of each. This influences how the interaction between the institutional aspects and the student voices play out and are foregrounded. Each institution has quality assurance barriers that exist. It is important that these are examined and that as a senior manager you work to ensure that colleagues understand that by reducing bureaucracy you are not taking risk. To encourage change you need to put alternatives forward that demonstrate that rather than potentially causing problems you are actually simplifying the situation.

Gill posited that where the literature often puts the two notions of enhancement and assurance as opposing forces (Filippakou & Tapper, 2008) this may be portraying things in a misguided form. She suggested that they are not necessarily mutually exclusive. Similar to the ways in which people often juxtapose research and teaching which may be unhelpful, the same can be said for quality enhancement and assurance. Rather she argued for recognising a symbiotic relationship between quality and learning outcomes and that within this comes the enhancement rather than seeing them as distinctly different activities (Williams, 2016). Similar to Dano and Stensaker (2007) Gill argued that they are linked and part of a continuous process and not therefore as distinct and separate. Within the quality structures that an institution has there are regulations and if these provide assessments that enhance the opportunities for the student to learn then they can work together and not in opposition. Gill suggested that often assessment does not however link to enhancement. Her experience suggests that there can be a danger that this relationship is not understood and if this occurs it draws in and establishes barriers to change which are then equated as extremes between on the one side enhancement and on the other quality assurance.

EARLY CAREER INFLUENCES

Having set the framework for the conversation we explored the influences on Gill through her own academic career. Initially Gill started as a student within science. She acknowledged that this influenced her future significantly. The notion of QED has remained central. She stated that theory is always there to be broken, to be re-looked at and examined (Kuhn, 2012). This approach, encountered as a student of science encouraged Gill to look at where an institution or team needed to get to and then work backwards to consider how to get there. The scientific approach taught her to examine what may not have gone as anticipated and to then go back and verify why it has gone wrong. In her experience she feels that this does not often happen in higher education. Instead people consider the immediacy of a problem and look for an immediate solution which actually may not be the most appropriate. In the scientific approach you look to see if the solution is feasible and whether the outcomes are appropriate for the future you are looking toward. In addition, Gill noted that it led her to a rational and systematic approach being adopted even though she acknowledged that there are aspects of emotion that come in because of the personal values that exist. The scientific approach however enabled her to mediate some of the stronger emotions that may at times otherwise lead to alternative decisions being made.

Reflecting back to her early career as a learner Gill noted that she was always keen to fulfil her potential and has subsequently had this as an important driver to enable others to be able to do the same. She stated that she believes that everyone should have that opportunity. When asked where this stemmed from she stated that she was often pushed to try things which appeared to be out of reach from an early age. She remembers being pushed at school although the learning environment was mostly about learning facts and doing as she was told. It was university that brought with it the notion that facts were no longer bare facts. As Whitehead (1959) said, they became infused with opportunity. This opened up for Gill an engagement with criticality and challenge. The ability to question '*why*' allows an individual to question, to ask for reasons which then provide an opportunity to open the world up. That was a fundamental change for Gill. Her undergraduate years brought that about and offered a new way of questioning. Undertaking a PhD provided an opportunity to learn that there was a particular way of writing and structuring work that allowed her to get a qualification. However, she felt that it was more about jumping through hoops and as a consequence was disappointing. By the time she completed her PhD she felt that whilst she had a capacity for criticality this had actually to some extent been limited. What it did offer however, was an avenue to explore other people and the way they approached problems and to be able to question these.

The move to the US provided renewed insight, demonstrating the importance of recognising where learning is situated (Brown et al., 1989). Here she found a much more open system that allowed her to question more and encouraged this in ways that she had not experienced before in the UK. That was a revelation. Taking the questions she had been perplexed by but finding a system that embraced these was a significant point in her own learning (Mezirow, 1997). This profound impact has not been forgotten and she noted that she has always tried to retain this and continues to try and bring this approach into her strategies for learning now.

As such this was a defining point. She realised that although she could ask questions there are sometimes boundaries which limit this. However, once you have the freedom and where you recognise that this exists, then you can question. There are potential challenges where the quality of the experience of the student can become bound by attempts to ensure that opportunities are available but that subsequently limits the creativity. This is particularly the case for higher areas of study. The conundrum is enabling the opportunity for fair opportunity so that people get support and at the same time allowing space for creativity as you go through the gateways of different learning and how people question in different ways.

Gill encountered these challenges having undertaken a social science oriented Masters programme. This provided her with different perspectives to those she encountered within science and the fusion allowed different questions to emerge. As a consequence Gill has tried to bring the two different approaches she learned together. In her experience the encouragement, or perhaps recognition of the value of such an interdisciplinary voice can be appreciated as it challenges a reductionist approach (DePryck, 1991). However, she noted that she has continued to experience scepticism that such an interdisciplinary way of thinking is of value.

COMPROMISE

Simon asked whether this had led to Gill having to compromise her values which underpin her actions (Inlow, 1972). Gill did not believe that it necessarily followed that she had to compromise her values. It has, she acknowledged, led to the need to fight for them and she accepted that she has not always won. Reflecting she said it was interesting that she does recognise compromise however at senior manager level. She explained that as an academic she does not compromise her values, she still writes and researches and will always fight for what she believes in through this work. The challenge comes particularly in management when you have to consider how you represent different values and develop them, appreciating that others will also have their own and that these will not always be in agreement given the significant potential range of backgrounds people represent. For Gill this does not mean dropping your own values. Rather it is about offering opportunities to engage in areas where perspectives can be provided and supported by evidence. The key to effective team working is that all those involved appreciate where it is that an institution is ultimately aiming for. At times this is not always comfortable and there are occasions it is extremely difficult. However, if there is an acknowledgement of where an organisation is aiming to get to and ways of achieving this can be found it does not follow that the underpinning values need to be compromised. It may be that they need to be shifted and allow a route to this which initially may not have been recognised. That, in many respects provides the real value of interdisciplinary working, enabling people to recognise multiple perspectives (Baloche et al., 1996).

Asked about an example Gill outlined how you may go about changing a regulatory framework at an institution. She stated that you are likely to find resistance. However, if your end point is that you want students to be able to fulfil their potential then the question becomes, how does the regulatory framework enable this? On examination you may find that the quality structure may not always allow this and as a result you need to engage the academic community. This is important so that they feel they can see that their learners can enhance what they do without reducing the quality of how they achieve this. Allowing the learner to achieve his or her potential is something that can be shared as an outcome. In her experience Gill believes that staff respond to evidence and when they find that through changes the learners get closer to achieving their potential, then they become supportive.

Simon asked whether such approaches may lead to a '*dumbing-down*' of approaches to student learning. Gill argued that this certainly does not need to be the case although she believed that at times this has occurred in the sector. This has happened she believes when there has been a lack of criticality; when the focus has been on the separation rather than the bringing together of the two elements of enhancement and quality. Where they are synthesised Gill argued there is greater opportunity for achievement, where the opportunity for the student to reach their potential occurs. Done well the structures allow the maximisation of the student learning and not separating the two. There is always externality that will ultimately demonstrate whether you have '*dumbed down*'. If you provide greater clarity about what a learner has to do you provide greater opportunity for them to then enhance and develop beyond.

THE ROLE OF TEACHING

The conversation then considered the role of teaching. Gill believes that there remains a tendency to perpetuate history through the teaching that many undertake. This she believes is not surprising. As teachers we use the frames of reference we have to develop ourselves and for many this will have been an inspiring teacher or variety of teachers who present the subject we then teach in a particular way, replicating the familiar (Mazur, 2009). Looking to the future is not always therefore undertaken which may create potential limitations in our teaching. For example, as we get older our learners remain the same age and therefore the differential increases. We need to try and understand the learning context within which the students are learning in rather than the context that we remember.

Exploring teaching in such a way can lead to misunderstanding and trying to talk to different communities in a large institution can exacerbate this further. Although Gill has been able to engage with different communities as a consequence of her own background and interdisciplinary work, this can also bring difficulty with the hybrid voice being developed that may not always be recognised if this is related solely by the recipient against his or her own background.

In response to this Gill argued for the importance of transparency, although she acknowledged that this can lead to misunderstanding. Rowland (2002) warned that this can lead to fragmentation both between academic staff and those managing them and also as a consequence of people shrinking within increasingly smaller disciplinary knowledge areas rather than seeking to transcend boundaries. That very '*concentratedness*' that Gill recognised is she feels potentially problematic. When teachers work exclusively within their own frames and conceive of the learning activity from within these boundaries this, whilst in many respects completely understandable, is potentially limiting. The same can be said when working at a more senior level and considering the broader strategic aims of the institution. This can present a real challenge. Gill argued that we need to acknowledge both and enable them to work together towards an aim that puts the student and her or his learning at the centre.

As Breakwell (1986) recognised such attempts to manage in such a way that transcends a particular approach can be seen to be offering a critique of it. This can cause a reaction that sees the approach as a threat because it challenges how a particular person or group conceive of the world. This can threaten the identity of that person or group. As a consequence those people who feel threatened often retrench within the disciplinary boundaries at a time when actually the '*risk*' that has been identified requires a new approach altogether (Beck, 1992).

Gill stated that in her experience in management, making space within the current pressures that exist is challenging. It is easier she noted to do what you are told to do and not take on the challenge of doing what you think might be right. This is something articulated by Parker Palmer in *The Courage to Teach* (1998) which Gill believes outlines this dilemma very well. The challenge presented can question our integrity and doing what an individual thinks is right may appear to challenge the trust and approach that an individual may ultimately be endeavouring to achieve. It can require a significant amount of trust to exist, and taking the '*risk*' is often not encouraged. Individuals often do not feel they have the trust of others to take such risk. Whilst the notion of '*intelligent failure*' (Sitkin, 1992) may be supported after the event it may often not be acknowledged in advance and subsequently people resort to a more limited approach and do not challenge the perceived orthodox.

As a teacher Gill always believed that the student and her learning was the focus. Ultimately this remains the case to this day. She stated that to enable this to work well you need a dialogue with them and it is a crucial relationship. She argued for the need to ensure that there is trust and that we behave as a community that is not in opposition (Fukuyama, 1996). If you examine why there is a lack of trust you can start to develop an evidence base then you can start to break down the mistrust. You have to be careful however not to go too far so that staff feel they are not trusted and create a division. If the balance goes too far then the trust becomes unbalanced again. There is a need to listen to the different voices, staff as well as student and within these groups the different voices that exist. She noted it is important to recognise that they all exist *within* the community and not externally. There are of course external voices, but colleagues and the students are internal. This relates to trust. Simon noted that within this is another potential challenge presented by the individual and the community because the university is a collective experience and yet the outcomes are often individual. Gill acknowledged that this can be problematic. The higher education environment does appear to reward the individual: the student gaining her degree or the staff member being given a promotion. Such a system may not sit well with how to envisage the notion of community and indeed may be more accentuated at certain places.

It was at this point in our conversation that Gill reflected on her own learning experience. She remembered being at school and Miss Potter telling her she could become an excellent historian but that she responded that she wanted to study science. She said that the passion she exhibited for history came from how Miss Potter made the subject come alive. That has lasted and it has always struck her how her love of science and that passion she retains for developing questions is always vulnerable. It can so easily be limited or reduced by the teaching of others. She says despite the vulnerability she retains that passion. She feels an emotional response to that ignition of her interest by Miss Potter and others when she listens to great teaching and yet how depressing it is when you hear a poor lecture or see a dull lab session. As the learning environment evolves Gill believes that the virtual environment offers opportunities to further ignite learners and this is a challenge to the sector: how do we enthuse the learner and ignite or keep alive that passion?

At this point Simon asked what impact efforts to professionalise teaching had made on the quality and enhancement of teaching within higher education. Gill said that she does not believe there is a simple answer to this. In her view teaching has changed and people have attempted to professionalise their approaches. What effect has this had and what can we learn from this and how institutions have approached this are complex. A cynical answer is that each initiative has been influenced by financial support and inducement and that has encouraged a set of behaviours or actions. Gill believes that even here an unforeseen consequence has been that improvement has actually happened. The limitation may be that we may not always have examined or fully been able to understand how the improvement actually occurred. So for example, is it making a league table that improved the learning, or was it the actual philosophy within the institution that altered and provided sustained change? During the conversation Gill noted that for her this is actually quite important and has helped to bring about improvements in the learning outcomes achieved by students. She warned however that whilst this sounds positive there is potentially, and from a philosophical perspective, a view that this is the wrong approach despite the positive outcome.

As academics we are brought up to question and to be critical, and therefore the notion of professionalising someone into the language and context that they do not understand may be mystifying to them. Gill argued that if we try to engage academics into the language of education we run the risk of not engaging them because the language is not familiar and it may appear irrelevant as a consequence. If you want engagement it seems entirely wrong to do this. However, if you take a psychological approach and consider what you need to do to make your students understand your love and passion for what you do in a way that they will understand then she believes it is more likely to work. This is why she says we may need to question and challenge approaches that push generic notions of education forward. In her view such an approach is unlikely to engage academic staff. It is about understanding that whilst there are generics it is the differences that are important and that we need to engage people with these so that it applies or becomes applicable and relevant to their practice. So for example, if we take a generic idea and help people see how it applies within their field and within their theoretical realm it comes with meaning. Gill argued that remaining in the generic is less likely to work because we are trying to invent and create a habitus (Bourdieu, 1986) that is imposed and draw people in. However, this is an entirely false construction. It is better to go into the academic's habitus, where the social understanding allows conversation that is recognisable and yet can be challenged and developed over time. Such an approach is likely to be seen as more relevant.

A SYMBIOTIC RELATIONSHIP

In her experience of observing institutions as they evolve Gill believes that some take a managerial approach that leads at times to separation of particular strands that are crucial to the work of the university. This can be based around the separation of teaching and research or the separation of quality enhancement and assurance rather than seeing the symbiotic relationship of the two. She believes that where you work to bring these together it can work very effectively. This she believes is where a senior management team need to focus their energies and work towards the drawing together of these elements to the advantage of both the institution and ultimately therefore the students. The senior managers need to provide and mirror these themselves and that can be challenging. The structures and approaches that are in place may have a profound impact upon this. To be a part of the broader community of academe is of potential importance. In the same way that a teacher who acknowledges with her students that she is a learner too creates an opportunity for a dialogue that is different from one who does not. So a senior manager who is still engaged in scholarship is similarly disposed to examine, to enquire, to question and acknowledge uncertainty. The alternative is a closed view that can limit how people within it respond. Gill argued that this can be damaging for an institution, and limit the potential of those working within it.

Gill acknowledged that different models exist and she finds this interesting. From her own experience of different institutional approaches they produce different sets of behaviour and influence the potential for criticality as a result. This is often influenced by external pressures as well which can highlight a particular aspect of the work of the institution. Rather than seeing the symbiotic relationship there can be an encouragement of either teaching or research at an institution. It may be that responses to external stimuli, such as league tables, encourage such a polarised approach (Hazelkorn, 2007).

At this point Simon asked what therefore success looks like. Gill considered this and replied that being successful requires an understanding of, and being able to take, an idea of where you need to be and how to get there. She reiterated that this can be problematic in a world where we are encouraged to see success in the short-term and to respond to the immediate. Although Gill herself has always tried to resist such responses herself she appreciates that others have different approaches and that she is responding based on her own methodology. From a senior managers perspective this is a case of where the institution needs to be and then to work backwards to see what the barriers are and where the gateways are that can facilitate this. Gill stated that this approach was instilled from her early work as a learner and reinforced as a scientist and as such it is how she has always worked as far as she is aware.

Relating this directly to learning and teaching she reflected on the development of a teaching and learning strategy. She stated that the end result was the development of a strategy that put the student at the centre. However, she was aware that not everyone was clear what such a strategy involved. As she considered this Gill recognised that not everyone was involved in teaching. However, they were all involved in learning. So she recognised that what she could base the work upon was the notion of learning and through this needed to consider what staff at the university do and do not do and that will and must involve the students. Talking to students was therefore crucial. Students told her that they often did not understand the language of policies and approaches and how this related to the teaching that they experienced. In the learning environment therefore we need to understand why and how the teachers work and how this can be understood. So whilst people were talking about teaching it was more important to focus on learning.

Reflecting further on this Gill argued that it is by seeing what the actual end point is that you can project what the current debates are leading towards. So for example, by projecting from teaching you get to learning. By the time people have shifted to talk about learning, the projection is about the student experience. For Gill, effective management is about starting the conversation and moving towards the end point and exploring what the actual question or debate is really asking. In the same way that people who teach and research forge new questions and draw people into these and move knowledge forward, so the process of managing in higher education is similar. It comes from asking and forming the next question and being interested in the unknown and thinking what the next question should be. This comes from a symbiotic approach. Rather than seeing the academic role as neatly divided between research and teaching, the approach is about drawing the two together to see that they are both involved in inquiry, about creating, asking and exploring the next question. This is opposed to seeing such an approach as the exclusive realm of research where exploration occurs and for teaching to be the preserve of the already '*known*'.

As a manager Gill reflected that the person who had the most significant influence was Harry. He had always talked to her about the what, the why and the where. What are we doing, why are we doing it and where do we need to get to. With experience Gill reflects that it is often the last question that is the one that needs the most thought. Questions then flow from this in terms of how and why. In her experience a lot of organisations do not fundamentally want to change. As a consequence it is often a case that management do not respond that well to questions that relate to change. Harry encouraged Gill to focus on where an institution needs to get to and then think about the strategies that allow you to get it there. She has learned that this does not mean that there is only one approach but it allows you to consider what the barriers are to enable you to get where you need to be. Currently the question has related to putting the student very much at the centre of the learning environment. That therefore has been the end point and as an institution it has been important to consider what the barriers have been to achieving this.

Thinking about what the next challenge may be Gill stated that it may be graduate employability and the student opportunity to graduate funding, or what their salaries are going to be. So in an institution it is important to think how to get to a point where this is the direction of travel and what are the barriers that need to be dealt with to achieve this. This may be looking at links with business, work placements and engaging with employers within the curriculum in more meaningful ways. This plays out within a learning and teaching strategy and how this needs to evolve to respond to that end point. So if, as may happen, people start to categorise university performance in part based on the salary and income of graduates then that becomes a potential end point which you can work back from.

This Gill was keen to point out, is not to suggest that a strategy requires a particular route that only leads to one outcome. For her an effective strategy allows different outcomes. It clearly helps if all the senior management team understand the strategic direction and that people begin to see how the strategic approach allows the aims that people have to be achieved. So in this case it is about enabling the student to be at the centre and a realisation that rather than limit the research opportunities of staff it can actually enhance them. An effective strategy is multi-layered and does not, if appropriately conceived mean that one approach is taken and that would limit the outcome.

CONCLUSION

Towards the end of the conversation Simon asked Gill to consider what she had learned from her experiences. Gill argued that from her perspective it is important never to devalue your own values. That is not to suggest they are more worthy; just that it is important to stay true to what you believe. To support this she said it is important to be clear in your thinking and be sure that you have your evidence available. She also noted that being strategic often meant that as a rule you do not speak first, instead you wait and listen. She revisited the notion of trust. She said that in her experience this is very important to demonstrate. Although you may often have this denied to you it is important to accept this but to remember that there are a significant number of people in an institution who are honest and trustworthy. These people provide opportunity to enable the direction being aimed for to be supported across and at different levels of the organisation. A recognition of this and using these people provides a far greater likelihood that success will be achieved. Gill acknowledged that within this there is significant complexity and that not all relationships will always work, however, when it does it is a real opportunity to make progress.

The pride that all staff and students can experience when this works is something that Gill believes is fundamental and lies at the heart of effective strategic pedagogic management. She reflected that it is a team approach and whilst senior management can have and put in place the vision, it will not work unless you have a team to enable that to be realised and achieved. Ultimately you need to trust a lot of people to do a lot of different tasks and then allow them to get on with what they do well and what they can bring to enable the barriers to be removed. It is a collective approach and that can be a problem in a large institution. There is a tendency to become fragmented on a variety of different levels, whether that is in terms of the discipline, the institution and where it is located and the different identities that exist within it. So whilst there may be one overall community, living within this there are potentially a lot of different communities existing who are all working towards potentially different targets and this can be problematic. However, higher education is a place where your abilities can and are tested and you can be stretched. You should always take the experiences and make the most of your previous learning opportunities and synthesise this knowledge and hopefully bring forward responses to these challenges. Gill believes that as a consequence she has learned to adapt because the context of each institution is very different. Whilst the ultimate aim may be the same, say to put the student at the centre, the challenge of each institution, the context, the visibility and identity, the behaviours, the structures, the history are all different. Some institutions are very embedded for example in their local community and others far less so. You therefore have to look at the potential barriers that exist as a consequence. The notion of community is really important and this can be recognised in different areas. It may be the student community, it may be the academic, the institutional or within the physical area. When these communities work in harmony towards the same end then it is effective and inevitably when they do not it is far less so.

REFERENCES

Baloche, L., Hynes, J., & Berger, H. (1996). Moving toward the integration of professional and general education. *Journal of Action in Teacher Education, 18*(1), 1–9.

Bates, E. A., & Kaye, L. K. (2014). I'd be expecting caviar in lectures: The impact of the new fee regime on undergraduate students' expectations of higher education. *Higher Education, 67*(5), 655–673.

Beck, U. (1992). *Risk society: Towards a new modernity.* London: Sage Publications.

Berliner, D. C. (1984). The half-full glass: A review of research on teaching. In P. L. Hosford (Ed.), *Using what we know about teaching* (pp. 51–85). Alexandria, VA: Association for Supervision and Curriculum Development.

Bourdieu, P. (1986). The forms of capital. In J. G. Richardson (Ed.), *Handbook of theory and research for the sociology of education* (pp. 241–258). New York, NY: Greenwood Press.

Breakwell, G. (1986). *Coping with threatened identities.* London: Methuen Publishing.

Brown, J. S., Collins, A., & Duguid, P. (1989). Situated cognition and the culture of learning. *Educational Researcher, 18*(1), 32–42.

Dano, T., & Stensaker, B. (2007). Still balancing improvement and accountability? Developments in external quality assurance in the Nordic countries 1996–2006. *Quality in Higher Education, 13*(1), 81–93.

DePryck, K. (1991). The challenge of interdisciplinarity. *Philisophica, 48*(2), 5–6.

Filippakou, O., & Tapper, E. (2008). Quality assurance and quality enhancement in higher education: Contested territories? *Higher Education Quarterly, 62*(1–2), 84–100.

Fukuyama, F. (1996). *Trust: Social virtues and the creation of prosperity.* New York, NY: Free Press.

Gall, M. D., Gall, J. P., & Borg, W. R. (2003). *Educational research: An introduction* (7th ed.). Boston, MA: A & B Publications.

Hazelkorn, E. (2007). The impact of league tables and ranking systems on higher education decision making. *Higher Education Management and Policy, 19*(2), 87–110.

Inlow, G. (1972). *Values in transition.* London: John Wiley & Sons.

Kuhn, T. (2012). *The structure of scientific revolutions* (4th ed., 50th anniversary ed./with an introductory essay by Ian Hacking). Chicago, IL: University of Chicago Press.

Lane, I. (2007). Change in higher education: Understanding and responding to individual and organisational resistance. *Journal of Veterinary Medical Education, 34*(2), 85–92.

Mazur, E. (2009). Farewell, lecture? *Science, 323*(5910), 50–51.

Mezirow, J. (1997). Transformative learning: Theory to practice. *New Directions for Adult and Continuing Education, 74*, 5–12.

Palmer, P. (1998). *The courage to teach: Exploring the inner landscape of a teacher's life.* San Francisco, CA: Jossey-Bass.

Rowland, S. (2002). Overcoming fragmentation in professional life: The challenge for academic development. *Higher Education Quarterly, 56*(1), 52–64.

Sitkin, S. (1992). Learning through failure: The strategy of small losses. *Research in Organisational Behavior, 14*, 231–266.

Stephenson, J., & Yorke, M. (1998). *Capability and quality in higher education.* London: Routledge.

Turner, D. (2010). Qualitative interview design: A practical guide for novice investigators. *The Qualitative Report, 15*(3), 754–760.

Whitehead, A. (1959). The aims of education. *Daedalus, 88*(1), 192–205.

Williams, J. (2016). Quality assurance and quality enhancement: Is there a relationship? *Higher Education Quarterly, 22*(2), 97–102.

Gill Nicholls (Retired)
University of Surrey
Guildford, UK

Simon Lygo-Baker
Department of Higher Education
University of Surrey
Guildford, UK

PAUL ASHWIN

8. BUILDING AN AGENDA FOR ACADEMIC DEVELOPMENT ON THE PECULIARITY OF UNIVERSITY TEACHING

INTRODUCTION

This book seeks to highlight the peculiarities of pedagogy through a series of dialogues between academics, academic developers and an institutional manager. The previous chapters have largely focused on what these dialogues can tell us about teaching in higher education. In this concluding chapter, I want to shift this focus to consider what these dialogues have highlighted about the peculiar nature of academic development. In exploring this, I write in dialogue with the preceding chapters, which I use as a jumping off point to explore the meaning of academic development and to develop an agenda for the kind of academic development that can support the enhancement of teaching and learning at an institutional and sector-wide level.

Peculiar Pedagogies

Before focusing on academic development, I want to briefly discuss the meaning of '*peculiarity*' within the notion '*pedagogic peculiarities*'. It has two main meanings: it can be a strange or unusual feature or it can be a distinctive characteristic. This means that '*pedagogic peculiarities in higher education*' can either refer to the strangeness of university teaching or to the distinctiveness of university teaching. Whilst these two senses may be related, the question '*What is distinctive about university teaching?*' seems a more usefully productive one than '*What is strange about university teaching?*' This is because whilst distinctiveness gives us a sense of something that is a necessary element of university teaching, being strange is something that is more defined by its difference to other types of activity. Thus in this concluding chapter I focus on the distinctiveness of university teaching, how this is discussed in the preceding chapters and the implications that these have for academic development in higher education.

THE DISTINCTIVENESS OF UNIVERSITY TEACHING

In thinking about the distinctiveness of university teaching, we can either consider how university teaching is distinctive from the other practices that academics engage in or the ways in which university teaching is a particular form of teaching. Whilst there is a body of literature that discusses the relations between teaching, research, administration and engagement within academic identity (see for example McAlpine & Åkerlind, 2010), there has been less discussion of how university teaching can be seen as a distinct form of teaching. It is this less discussed distinctiveness of university teaching that I focus on in this chapter.

We can get a sense of this kind of distinctiveness by comparing university teaching to teaching in other formal educational settings such as nurseries, schools, and vocational colleges. One useful way of doing this is through Basil Bernstein's (2000) notion of the '*pedagogic device*'. The pedagogic device brings together the way in which knowledge is differentially distributed (distribution rules), made available for teaching through the production of curricula (recontextualising rules), and is transformed into ways of assessing students' performances (evaluation rules) (Bernstein, 2000; Singh, 2002; Ashwin, 2009). It can be seen as providing a sense of three forms of knowledge: the distribution rules can be seen as focusing on knowledge-as-research; the recontextualising rules on knowledge-as-curriculum and the evaluation rules on knowledge-as-student-understanding (Ashwin, 2014).

Whilst it is important to be clear that the pedagogic device operates at the level of societies rather than individual institutions, it highlights that what is peculiar about universities as educational institutions is that all three forms of knowledge are produced within a single institution. Thus academics collectively produce knowledge-as-research, they also design degree programmes and thus produce knowledge-as-curriculum, and they teach these programmes to students and help to produce knowledge-as-student-understanding. This makes university teaching distinct from teaching in other educational institutions; in which curriculum are usually defined outside of the institution by qualification bodies, professional associations or government agencies and in which those teaching tend not to be contributing, through research, to the body of knowledge that they are teaching.

Another important element of the pedagogic device is that knowledge is transformed as it moves from knowledge-as-research to knowledge-as-curriculum and to knowledge-as-student-understanding. As Kinchin, Kingsbury and Buhmann show in their chapter, the differences between these forms of knowledge can be seen in the ways that different understandings of the same idea or concept are held by undergraduate students, masters' students and university teachers.

Crucially the transformation of knowledge as it moves between the different rules of the pedagogic device means that as the form of knowledge changes, so the logic that informs that form of knowledge changes. Thus, as Bernstein (2000) argues, this means that the logic of the curriculum is not the same as the logic of the discipline. This is because the process of producing curricula is conflictual with different agents seeking to define which elements of a discipline or professional field are included as part of a curriculum. In universities, this involves discussions between agents such as academics, professional bodies, institutional quality agents, external examiners, national quality agencies etc. (Ashwin, 2009). Power plays a crucial role in this process, for example the power of senior staff and that of accreditation agencies to impose their view of the defining elements of the professional field, as Hosein and Harle show in their chapter. In this way, the discipline is transformed as it is turned into a particular curriculum. Similarly when students engage with that curriculum, they transform the knowledge themselves as they relate it to their previous knowledge and experiences (see Ashwin, 2009 for a fuller discussion of this process).

In the remainder of this chapter I consider the implications of this peculiar feature of university teaching, as well as the contributions to this book, for how we think about university teaching and academic development in universities. I do this by examining a series of tensions that are raised by this way of thinking that have important implications for how we understand the nature of academic development. In conclusion, I argue that these implications form a coherent, holistic and challenging agenda for the future of academic development.

TENSION 1: BETWEEN TEACHING AS AN INDIVIDUAL AND TEACHING AS A COLLECTIVE ACTIVITY

As Stephen Brookfield outlines with the notion of '*alone whilst not alone*' in his introduction to this book, teaching is often thought about as an individual activity even though it is embedded in collective networks. Thinking of teaching in terms of the pedagogic device brings the collective nature of teaching into the foreground. It highlights the ways in which academics draw on collective knowledge when they design curricula, a process which itself is undertaken by groups of academics and other agents. Students themselves tend to experience programmes as a collective whole rather than as individual modules. Even when someone teaches and assesses an entire module alone, they draw upon knowledge that has been collectively produced and seek to evaluate students' levels of understanding of this collective knowledge.

However, despite the essentially collective nature of university teaching, most of the ways in which such teaching is assessed and developed treats it as an individual activity. Most forms of academic development focus on developing individual teachers, largely through teaching qualifications, rather than working with course teams to collectively develop curricula. Awards for teaching are often individually focused and highlight the popular idea of the individual teacher who changes lives forever (for example in a University College Union campaign https://www.ucu.org.uk/article/2568/Power-of-education-unleashed-through-UCUs-first-Life-Changer-grants). This focus often means that problems are seen in terms of poor individual performance rather than as issues of problematic curriculum design. Classic examples of this are discussions of how to improve students' experiences of feedback. Results from student surveys internationally suggest that students do not perceive they receive enough feedback during their undergraduate degrees (for example, see Scott, 2014). As Scott (2014) shows, university teachers, and I would add institutions, often see this as a problem of students not understanding what feedback is, which will be resolved by individual academics making it more explicit

115

when they are providing feedback. However, it is more productively thought about as a problem of poor curriculum design. We do not design our curricula so that students are asked to use the feedback they have received to develop their work further. If students do not use feedback to improve their work, then it is difficult to see how this activity can be considered to constitute feedback. The answer then is to redesign curricula so that this becomes central to the way courses are designed.

This tension between the individual and collective nature of teaching highlights the question of what should be the focus of academic development. Academic developers' main institutional responsibility tends to be to provide courses for new academics from across their institution, which gives these new academics access to the principles of good teaching and assessment. However, these academics have little or no power or credibility to redesign curricula in their departments and instead tend to adopt the ways of teaching of their more established colleagues (Fanghanel, 2012), as Nicholls and Lygo recognise in their chapter. This is not to suggest that supporting individual academics to develop their teaching is not important, clearly all university teachers need time and space to develop their teaching. Rather it is to argue that this will not lead to sustained changes to university teaching, without also supporting programme teams within academic departments and helping to ensure that they have the time and space to question the design of their courses. Convincing senior university managers and academic departments that such, apparently, resource heavy strategic academic development is the only sustainable path to improved university teaching is difficult but is necessary if academic development is to successfully aim at institutional level changes to the quality of university teaching.

TENSION 2: BETWEEN THE LOCAL AND THE GLOBAL IN TEACHING

The second tension is between the local and the global in university teaching and is linked to the first tension in many ways. Lee Shulman's (1987) notion of pedagogical content knowledge gives a good sense of how the local and global come together in teaching. This notion positions the expertise of teaching as being able to understand how to make particular aspects of knowledge accessible to particular groups of students. This notion is helpful because it highlights the ways in which teaching is not simply student-centred or knowledge-centred but is rather about designing ways in which to bring students into a productive relationship to knowledge. Whilst this may seem in contrast to the emphasis on putting students at the centre in Nicholls and Lygo-Baker's chapter, they do this as a way of considering how to move students into engagement with knowledge and how to give the student the best opportunity to be successful within their learning environment. This is consistent with pedagogical content knowledge's focus on both what the material is and how we can configure it to make it accessible to the particular students that we are working with. Importantly, this is not about an idealised student or an abstract notion of knowledge but rather about thinking about particular students and how they can gain access to particular forms of knowledge. This clearly reinforces the centrality of curriculum design in teaching discussed under the first tension.

This means that a critical aspect of the curriculum design process is to design ways in which to make particular forms of knowledge accessible to particular students. It also highlights a new role for academic developers in helping programme teams think through ways of making knowledge accessible to their students. The potential complexity of this process is outlined in Hosein and Harle's chapter, in which they show how the nature of who students are can change the focus of a course. In the one year Masters' programmes in Medical Physics, there were students from a variety of academic disciplines, which presented challenges about how to take account of students' different knowledge bases. This was very different from the three year masters course in which students are practitioners within the NHS.

As part of this curriculum design process, there is also a need to understand students' expectations of their roles and responsibilities. Watermeyer and Tomlinson's chapter offers a dark vision of students' expectations having shifted to that of a consumer of qualifications. However, Ashwin and McVitty (2015) argue that this is more to do with a disjunction between the ways in which students are invited to engage with their institutions and the reality of the limits that are set on such engagement. Often the rhetoric of institutions implies that students are partners in the teaching-learning processes, in developing curricula and in developing the community of their institutions. Too often what happens in practice is that students are merely consulted and given choices between carefully pre-defined options rather than offered an authentic say in the development of the academic community of which they are part. It is this disjunction between rhetoric and reality that can lead students to focus on their role of consumers. To be clear, this is not to imply that students have the same role as academics in such partnerships. The role played by any partner needs to be defined by the knowledge and expertise that they bring to the particular object of engagement: whether this be the teaching-learning process, the development of curricula or the development of communities.

This nicely highlights the question of the nature of expertise that academic developers bring to the curriculum design process and their engagement with academic staff. As Pesata and Barrie (2017) argue, too often this expertise is positioned in terms of knowledge about how students learn rather than in terms of knowledge of how to support others to learn how to teach or knowledge of how to develop teaching at an institutional level. In this way the tension between local and global highlights the need for academic developers to have a clear sense of the basis of their expertise if they are to have the credibility to help to support programme teams to develop their curricula in the ways discussed under the first tension.

TENSION 3: BETWEEN COMPLEXITY AND SIMPLIFICATION

In his introduction Brookfield highlights the complexity of being a teacher; the ways in which plans change when they are implemented in practice. Brookfield's response to such complexity is that we need to recognise the importance of '*muddling through*' and to recognise the complex multiplicity and unpredictability of teaching-learning interactions. Whilst Brookfield is undoubtedly right about the complexity of teaching and learning interactions, the question that remains is how we respond to such complexity. How do we do more than say '*Well, it's complicated?*'

The chapter by Medland, James and Bailey offers one way of responding, with the notion of '*messy precision*'. This is described by a theatre designer as the ability to make models and build sets whilst also being able to respond reflexively to complexity. As I have argued before (Ashwin, 2009), in recognising that the complexity of the world exceeds our capacity to know it, we have to accept that our plans and strategies are based on simplifications of the world. Different ways of simplifying are based on different assumptions about the social world and so will not be compatible. This means that it is not possible to synthesise all simplifications together and attempts at such synthesis will lead to oversimplifications of the social world (Mol & Law, 2002). Rather, as Mol and Law (2002) argue:

> It becomes instead a matter of determining which simplification or simplifications we will attend to and create and, as we do this, of attending to what they foreground and draw attention to, as well as what they relegate to the background. (p. 11)

However, as Strathern (2002) argues, it is possible to shift between these different simplifications in order to examine what understanding of a situation is offered by their different foci.

Dealing with the complexity of university teaching requires us to attend to the ways in which we understand teaching situations. Part of this, as I argued above, is that we need to recognise that such understandings are not individual but are collectively produced. If we are to develop a deeper understanding of university teaching, we need to allow our simplifications to be challenged and developed by messy reality. This involves developing models of reflective teaching (see Ashwin et al., 2015) that recognise, as Brookfield argues in his introduction, the situated, emotional and intellectual character of university teaching. However, it also involves drawing on evidence about our practices and discussing this with others in order to make sense of it. Finally, we have to recognise, that in the end, we have to make judgements as teachers and these will always be based on interpretations of this evidence and on simplified understandings of university teaching.

For academic development, this means that we need to help university teachers to develop a '*modesty*' (Law, 2004) and provisional-ness about their teaching whilst also having the same attitude to our own practices. We also need to help university teachers to understand teaching as something that is developed collectively and in which there is no certainty of '*best practice*' to fall back on. Rather we need to help to develop university teachers who take responsibility for making judgements that are uncertain but are based on strong evidence about their teaching practices and research-informed simplifications of university teaching. Part of this, as Kinchin,

Kingsbury and Buhmann show in their chapter, is to invite academics to engage in investigations of their teaching. They illustrate an approach that authentically integrates the assessment of learning with the production of knowledge through research. In this way, the tension between complexity and simplification highlights a particular kind of relationship between academic developers and university teachers, which involves supporting university teachers to make difficult collective judgements. Such relationships are not possible without a clear sense of the expertise of academic development discussed under the second tension.

TENSION 4: BETWEEN THE PRACTICAL AND THEORETICAL

In their chapter, Medland, James and Bailey highlight the tensions, within the performing arts, between the academic nature of drama and the performance-focused nature of acting. They argue that this leads to tensions between the ways in which departments present their practices and the ways in which they enact those practices. In their chapter, Hosein and Harle highlight that even within the same apparent qualification, the practical and theoretical can be positioned in different ways. They contrast the one-year full time and three-year part time Masters' programmes in Medical Physics. With the one year programme being much more '*pure*' and academically focused and the three year part time programme for NHS practitioners being much more applied. These programmes lead to different identities for medical physicists that either a researcher or device specialist in industry or a healthcare scientist in a hospital.

These kinds of tensions are also evident in academic development practices. I have already discussed the tendency for academic developers to focus on providing new academics with introductory courses on university teaching. These courses can sometimes focus on theoretical models of best practice whilst remaining remote from the day-to-day demands and compromises of teaching. There is a real challenge of how to get the right balance between hints and tips for survival and ways of promoting a career-long fascination with teaching ones subject and ones students (Ashwin et al., 2015). The tension between the practical and theoretical raises similar questions about the nature of identity that academic developers are trying to encourage in the academics that they are working with. What kind of university teachers are academic developers trying to develop? Answering this question is made more difficult because of the lack of an organised body of knowledge of academic development and the variety of paths to becoming an academic developer (Peseta & Barrie, 2017).

TENSION 5: BETWEEN IDEAS OF WHAT IT MEANS TO BE AN ACADEMIC

In different ways, the chapters in this book identify a number of different understandings of what it means to be a contemporary academic. Hosein and Harle argue that academics should be focused on finding pedagogies that meet the needs of their students. Watermeyer and Tomlinson's chapter offers a darker view of academic identity in which '*competitive accountability*' dominates the practices of academics. In this vision, academics are overly keen to sell their expertise and knowledge in response to externally determined agendas, such as societal impact and research and teaching excellence. This produces a bleak vision of what it means to be professional, in which both students and academics are simply focused on the transactional production of educational outcomes rather than a politically-informed project. However, it should be said that this seems to be set against a higher education past that never existed. Thus whilst Watermeyer and Tomlinson write of the '*emergence of conformist pedagogy*', there seems to be very little evidence that the radical past they refer to ever existed on a systemic level. It is also important to be clear that narratives of the great decline have always been with us, as has the sense that students and academics were not what they were (for example, see Tight, 2010). The tendency to feel that one entered academia at just the wrong time, when the great freedoms and privileges have diminished, is one that must be resisted if one is not to fall into self-indulgent despair.

This dystopian vision of professionalism is greatly at odds with that offered through the dialogue of Young and Lygo-Baker. In this dialogue, we are given a rich sense of someone committed to their discipline and their teaching and to developing a guiding sense of professionalism. In this way, this tension between types of academic identity raises questions about the identity and professionalism of academic developers. Views on the professionalism of academic developers will be informed by the issues discussed above, such as the focus of academic development, the nature of expertise of academic developers, their relationships with academic staff, and the kinds of academics they are seeking to produce. Peseta and Barrie (2017) argue that a key element of the professionalism of academic development requires that newcomers to the field of academic development are inducted into an ethic of care for the field, which they argue can be captured by the notion of '*stewardship*'.

TENSION 6: BETWEEN EXCELLENCE AND ENHANCEMENT

Whilst Nicholls and Lygo-Baker's dialogue focuses on the tension between enhancement and assurance, what comes across from the book as a whole is the tension between enhancement and excellence. Watermeyer and Tomlinson's chapter convincingly highlights some of the dangers of overly focusing on excellence; in particular, the ways in which it leads to false and inflated claims in relation to teaching and research. The dangers of the language of excellence become even clearer when it is contrasted with the idea of enhancement. Whilst both involve comparisons, the language of enhancement is about comparing past and present practices in order to show how those practices have been improved. In contrast, excellence is simply about being better than others; it doesn't matter if your practices get worse providing they are better than those you are compared with. This means that excellence is always about competing with others in the sector and showing you are better rather than supporting enhancement of teaching across the sector. This downside of excellence is highlighted in Hosein and Harle's chapter, when they show how such competition prevents the sharing of practice across institutions in medical physics.

The tension between excellence and enhancement raises the question for academic developers of how they should respond if they are located in a university that prioritises excellence over enhancement. This question highlights the nature of the relationship between academic developers and the senior management of their institution. If academic developers have a professional commitment to enhancement then they may need to find ways to challenge the dominant thinking about teaching excellence within their institution rather than simply seeing themselves as the implementers of institutional policy (see Roxå & Mårtensson, 2017). This involves recognising that there are differences in the perspectives of academic developers and that of the institution, as Nicholls and Lygo-Baker show about Gill's different identities as a researcher and an institutional manager. This does not mean that they are necessarily in conflict but academic developers do need to recognise that they are different. This points to the need for academic developers to position themselves as leaders of teaching enhancement in their institutions and to draw on their expertise and commitment to support the development of particular kinds of academic identities in order to show university managers the benefits to their institution of pursuing an enhancement agenda. This kind of leadership is discussed by Nicholls and Lygo-Baker. It is one in which academic developers offer a strategic vision of how university teaching might be enhanced. A strategic vision that can be achieved through a variety of approaches and lead to a variety of outcomes but all of which are underpinned by strong values, trust, robust evidence and a clear sense of the community that is being supported.

TENSION 7: BETWEEN THE RADICAL POTENTIAL OF UNIVERSITY TEACHING AND THE TENDENCY FOR CONFORMITY IN UNIVERSITY TEACHING

The final tension is between the radical potential of university teaching and its tendency for conformity, which is discussed in the chapters by Young and Lygo-Baker and by Watermeyer and Tomlinson. This tension arises because, as discussed earlier, academics play a much more prominent role in designing the curricula and forms of assessment on the programmes they teach than teachers in any other educational setting. This means that they have a remarkable degree of freedom to design radical ways in which to help students to develop an understanding of their disciplines and professional fields. This freedom is even inscribed in notions of academic freedom that protect academics to teach their disciplines in ways that they feel are appropriate (Altbach, 2001). And yet there is a general sense of university teaching being traditional and conservative (Jääskelä et al., 2017). There still appear to be the credibility issues for those who take their teaching seriously; the risk, identified by Bourdieu et al. (1996), of 'appearing as a primary school teacher who has strayed into higher education' (p. 14). Indeed some academics rail against the very notion that what they engage in is teaching, choosing to describe it as lecturing and their job as simply to know their field (see Elton, 2006).

One of the areas in which this conservatism is most evident is in the assessment methods used in higher education. Whilst many claim this is due to disciplinary differences in modes of assessment, which reflect the different knowledge structures of the disciplines (see Trowler, 2014), the pedagogic device reminds us that the logic of the discipline does not determine the logic of the curriculum. Similarly, some studies have found that institutional setting plays a stronger role in determining assessment approach than disciplinary setting (Gibbs & Dunbar-Goddet, 2009). The problems of such institutional conformity are illustrated in the chapter by Medland, James and Bailey. They highlight the inability of assessment to take account of the continuous nature of performance in the performing arts because they focus on the products that students generate rather than the processes by which they are generated. This provokes a challenge of translating authentic assessment in this discipline area into the standardised language of the institution. However, these are not only challenges in the dramatic arts. In their chapter, Young and Lygo-Baker discuss similar challenges in assessing professional competence, in particular the processes involved in decision making as a vet and the importance of being able to make provisional judgements that are open to reinterpretation and change as knowledge of the situation changes.

How should academic development engage with such conservatism and attempt to open-up the potential of university teaching? The challenge for academic developers is that because they are largely positioned as general experts on teaching and learning, they are not in a position to challenge academics to produce curricula that are more radical interpretations of how to bring students into relation to powerful knowledge. As Nicholls and Lygo-Baker explore in their chapter, this highlights the need to move beyond the generic, so that academic developers engage with university teachers in order to explore their particular disciplines and professional fields. This kind of engagement can only be successful if academic developers have academic credibility. Thus academic development needs to be scholarly (Ashwin & Trigwell, 2004) and engage in genuine dialogue with university teachers about the most effective ways of making disciplinary and professional knowledge accessible to their particular students. Such engagement is not new: for example, the literature around phenomenography and threshold concepts are largely based on collaborations between academic developers and academic staff focused on understanding the different ways that students understand particular concepts in an attempt to improve student learning (for example see Prosser & Trigwell, 1999; Land et al., 2008). Whilst such work is not new, there is a danger that this history is forgotten in the obsession with the new ways of understanding academic development, which can cause us to lose sight of the existing collective body of knowledge of academic development (Ashwin, 2017).

CONCLUSION

In conclusion, I suggest that the contributions to this book can be seen to highlight the crucial role that academic development plays in supporting the development of less conformist approaches to university teaching. These approaches should put the peculiar feature of university teaching, that knowledge-as-research, knowledge-as-curriculum and knowledge-as-student-understanding all exist in a single institution, at their centre. This involves carefully designing environments and experiences that bring students into a productive relationship to powerful knowledge.

It is important to be clear that supporting the development of such approaches is difficult. It will be an ongoing process that is not all-or-nothing but rather about degrees of success, which are built upon learning from times when things do not work. To be successful, there is a need for an approach to academic development that is rooted in the seven tensions that I have identified in this chapter. In relation to the first tension, this involves a focus on collective practices and curriculum design that will lead to institutional change rather than a focus solely on changing individual teachers. In relation to the second tension, this involves a clear sense on the expertise of academic developers which helps to develop the kinds of relationship with university teachers that was highlighted under the third tension. Together these help to create a clear sense of the kind of university teachers that academic developers are seeking to develop, which was discussed under the fourth tension. The fifth tension shifted to focus on the identity of academic developers which led to a different relationship with their institutions and the need for academic developers to be leaders, as discussed under the sixth tension. Finally the seventh tension highlighted the importance of the academic credibility of academic developers that needed to be underpinned by a scholarly approach to academic development. This shows how the seven tensions highlight a coherent, holistic and challenging agenda for the future development of academic development.

REFERENCES

Altbach, P. (2001). Academic freedom: International realities and challenges. *Higher Education, 41*(1), 205–219.
Ashwin, P. (2009). *Analysing teaching-learning interactions in higher education: Accounting for structure and agency.* London: Continuum.
Ashwin, P. (2014). Knowledge, curriculum and student understanding. *Higher Education, 67*, 123–126.
Ashwin, P. (2017). Theorising learning to teach: Insights, absences, and future possibilities. In B. Leibowitz, V. Bozalek, & P. Khan (Eds.), *Theorising learning to teach in higher education.* London: Routledge.
Ashwin, P., Boud, D., Coate, K., Hallett, F., Keane, E., Krause, K.-L., Leibowitz, B., MacLaren, I., McArthur, J., McCune, V., & Tooher, M. (2015). *Reflective teaching in higher education.* London: Bloomsbury Academic.
Ashwin, P., & McVitty, D. (2015). The meanings of student engagement: Implications for policies and practices. In A. Curaj, L. Matei, R. Pricopie, J. Salmi, & P. Scott (Eds.), *The European higher education area* (pp. 343–359). Cham: Springer International Publishing. Retrieved from http://link.springer.com/chapter/10.1007%2F978-3-319-20877-0_23
Ashwin, P., & Trigwell, K. (2004). Investigating educational development. In D. Baume & P. Kahn (Eds.), *Enhancing staff and educational development.* London: Kogan Page.
Bernstein, B. (2000). *Pedagogy, symbolic control and identity: Theory, research and critique* (Revised ed.). Lanham, MD: Rowman and Littlefield Publishers.
Bourdieu, P., Passeron, J.-C., & de Saint-Martin, L. (1996). *Academic discourse: Linguistic misunderstanding and professional power* (R. Teese, Trans.). Cambridge: Polity Press.

Elton, L. (2006). The nature of effective or exemplary teaching in an environment that emphasizes strong research and teaching links. *New Directions for Teaching and Learning, 20*, 33–41. doi:10.1002/tl.243

Fanghanel, J. (2012). *Being an academic*. London: Routledge.

Gibbs, G., & Dunbar-Goddet, H. (2009). Characterising programme-level assessment environments that support learning. *Assessment & Evaluation in Higher Education, 34*(4), 481–489.

Jääskelä, P., Häkkinen, P. & Rasku-Puttonen, H. (2017) Supporting and constraining factors in the development of university teaching experienced by teachers. *Teaching in Higher Education, 22*(6), 655–671.

Land, R., Meyer, J. H. F., & Smith, J. (Eds.). (2008). *Threshold concepts within the disciplines*. Rotterdam, The Netherlands: Sense Publishers.

Law, J. (2004). *After method: Mess in social science research*. London: Routledge.

McAlpine, L., & Åkerlind, G. (Eds.). (2010). *Becoming an academic: International perspectives*. Basingstoke: Palgrave Macmillan.

Mol, A., & Law, J. (2002). Complexities: An introduction. In J. Law & A. Mol (Eds.), *Complexities: Social studies of knowledge practices*. Durham, NC: Duke University Press.

Pesata, T., & Barrie, S. (2017). Stewardship as practice: 'Learning of the job' for the academic developer newcomer. In B. Leibowitz, V. Bozalek, & P. Khan (Eds.), *Theorising learning to teach in higher education*. London: Routledge.

Prosser, M., & Trigwell, K. (1999). *Understanding learning and teaching: The experience in higher education*. Buckingham: Society for Research into Higher Education and Open University Press.

Roxå, T., & Mårtensson, K. (2017). Agency and structure in academic development practices: Are we liberating academic teachers or are we part of a machinery supressing them? *International Journal for Academic Development, 22*(2), 95–105.

Scott, S. (2014). Practising what we preach: Towards a student-centred definition of feedback. *Teaching in Higher Education, 19*(1), 49–57.

Shulman, L. (1987). Knowledge and teaching: Foundations of the new reform. *Harvard Educational Review, 57*, 1–23.

Singh, P. (2002). Pedagogising knowledge: Bernstein's theory of the pedagogic device. *British Journal of Sociology of Education, 23*(4), 571–582.

Strathern, M. (2002). On space and depth. In J. Law & A. Mol (Eds.), *Complexities: Social studies of knowledge practices*. Durham, NC: Duke University Press.

Tight, M. (2010). The golden age of academe: Myth or memory? *British Journal of Educational Studies, 58*(1), 105–116.

Trowler, P. (2014). Depicting and researching disciplines: Strong and moderate essentialist approaches. *Studies in Higher Education, 39*(10), 1720–1731.

Paul Ashwin
Department of Educational Research
Lancaster University
Lancashire, UK

ABOUT THE CONTRIBUTORS

Paul Ashwin is Professor of Higher Education and Head of the Department of Educational Research, Lancaster University, UK. Paul's research focuses on teaching–learning and knowledge–curriculum practices in higher education and their relations to higher education policies. Paul's books include *Analysing Teaching-Learning Interactions in Higher Education* (2009, Continuum) and *Reflective Teaching in Higher Education* (2015, Bloomsbury). Paul is a researcher in the ESRC and HEFCE-funded Centre for Global Higher Education, a coordinating editor for the international journal *Higher Education*, and co-editor of the Bloomsbury book series *Understanding Student Experiences of Higher Education*.

Niall Bailey is an accomplished Musical Supervisor, Director and Composer who works internationally and in London. He is currently Senior Musical Director at the Guildford School of Acting where he works on the undergraduate and postgraduate Musical Theatre and Acting programmes and is also a senior tutor on the new Actor Musician undergraduate course.

Stephen D. Brookfield is the John Ireland Endowed Chair at the University of St. Thomas in Minneapolis-St. Paul. He has worked over five decades in community, adult and higher education in Britain, Canada and the United States. Informed by European critical theory and American pragmatism, he is engaged in the experimental pursuit of beautiful consequences and interested in learning about, and helping others fight against, ideological manipulation. His work within and outside the academy focuses on teaching critical thinking, democratizing the classroom, and understanding the responsible use of teacher power. You can contact him via his website: www.stephenbrookfield.com

Stefan Yoshi Buhmann is an Emmy Noether Fellow and Junior Fellow of the Freiburg Institute for Advanced Studies, leading a research group in Macroscopic Quantum Electrodynamics at the Institute of Physics at the Albert-Ludwigs-University of Freiburg. He is the author of two monographs on dispersion forces. Having received a MEd in University Learning and Teaching at Imperial College London, his research interests in education are concept mapping, threshold concepts and the use of philosophy of science in physics teaching.

Jamie Harle is a graduate of Imperial College London (Physics) and specialised in medical physics, at the University of Oxford (MSc and DPhil). After postdoctoral work at UCL, he completed medical physicist hospital training at Cambridge University Hospitals NHS Trust. He has worked at The Open University, The

University of Liverpool and UCL. He is the programme director of the UCL MSc in Physics and Engineering in Medicine. Jamie was the recipient of the UCL Provost's Award for Leadership and Impact in Teaching and the University of London Centre for Distance Education (CDE) Teaching & Research Award. He is interested in the pedagogical practice of healthcare professionals and industry experts.

Anesa Hosein is a Lecturer in the Department of Higher Education at the University of Surrey. She is a Senior Fellow of the Higher Education Academy and member of the Research & Development Committee for the Society for Research into Higher Education (SRHE). She has worked in the higher education systems of the Caribbean and in the UK. She has an eclectic collection of qualifications and an equally eclectic collection of research namely in academic practice, mathematics education, research methods pedagogy, educational technology and migrant academics.

Alison James is Director of Academic Quality and Development and Professor of Learning and Teaching at the University of Winchester. She is also a National Teaching Fellow and a Principal Fellow of the Higher Education Academy in the UK. She has worked in creative arts education in a variety of guises, across all levels and many subjects – as educational and staff developer, researcher and policy maker and teacher. Her trademark is creative and interactive approaches to pedagogy and she is widely published on these, with particular emphasis on play, individual narratives of learning and alternative modes of critical reflection. She is an accredited LEGO® SERIOUS PLAY® facilitator and uses the method widely in HE

Ian M. Kinchin is Professor of Higher Education in the Department of Higher Education at the University of Surrey. Ian has published research in the fields of zoology, science education and academic development. He is the editor of the Journal of Biological Education; a Fellow of the Royal Society of Biology; a Senior Fellow of the Higher Education Academy, and is a member of the Governing Council of the Society for Research into Higher Education. He was an external examiner at Imperial College London between 2012 and 2016.

Martyn Kingsbury is Director of Educational Development and Head of the Educational Development Unit (EDU) at Imperial College London. He comes from a biomedical background but an MA in education and a growing interest in pedagogy led him into educational development in 2005 and he has been running the EDU since 2010. In addition to managing the unit he teaches and supervises students at all stages of the EDU's flexible three stage Master's in University Learning and Teaching programme. His research interests include concept mapping, self-efficacy, authenticity and the academic prestige economy in research-focused higher education.

ABOUT THE CONTRIBUTORS

Simon Lygo-Baker is Head of the Department of Higher Education at the University of Surrey. He also holds a visiting position at the School of Veterinary Medicine, University of Wisconsin-Madison. He completed a Masters in Political Science at Warwick University before undertaking a PhD in Education looking at identity and values in university teaching. As a university teacher he initially worked on a range of projects working with marginalised communities such as refugees and asylum seekers and those in recovery from addiction. More recently he has worked at King's College London and the University of Surrey working in academic development and researching aspects of learning and teaching within the disciplines.

Emma Medland is a Lecturer in Higher Education with the Department of Higher Education at the University of Surrey. She is a Senior Fellow of the Higher Education Academy, a member of the Society for Research into Higher Education's Research and Development Committee, and has been a Lecturer in Higher Education for ten years, working at Surrey and King's College London. Her current role focuses on the provision of Continuing Professional Development to support the pedagogic development of academic staff and those involved in supporting learning across the institution. Emma's research interests lie in assessment and feedback and academic practice in higher education.

Gill Nicholls until recently was the Vice President and Deputy Vice-Chancellor for Academic Affairs at the University of Surrey. Gill has also held senior management positions at the University of Salford, University of Durham, and King's College London. Over the years Gill has worked with a range of national advisory groups and committees including HEFCE Teaching Excellence and Student Opportunity Advisory Committee, the Council of the All-Party Parliamentary University Group, she is currently a member of the TEF panel, and in December 2015 received the OBE for her services to Higher Education.

Michael Tomlinson is an Associate Professor within Southampton Education School at the University of Southampton. He was previously a lecturer at Keele University in the School of Public Policy and Professional Practice. Following an ESRC-funded doctorate and ESRC post-doctoral fellowship in the School of Social Sciences at Cardiff University, he worked on a large-scale ESRC-funded project at the Cardiff Business School exploring leadership and leadership development in the public services. His research is located broadly within the sociology of education and work, particularly in relation to the changing context and nature of work and its impact on people's identities and approaches to work and careers. More specific research interests lie in the higher education and labour market interplay and the social construction of 'graduate employability'. Within this area, his research has explored transitions from higher education to work and how employability is constructed and managed by students and graduates. He is also interested in graduates' early career experiences and their engagement in processes of work-related learning and skill formation.

ABOUT THE CONTRIBUTORS

Richard Watermeyer is a Reader in Education at the University of Bath. He is by training and orientation a sociologist of education, knowledge, science and expertise. His interests broadly encompass issues of educational policy, practice and pedagogy. He is specifically engaged in critical studies of higher education and the changing nature of academic identity and practice. He has held academic appointments at the universities of Cardiff, Surrey and Warwick and was the first social scientist to be seconded to the Office of the Chief Scientific Adviser for Wales.

Karen Young received her VMD and PhD from the University of Pennsylvania in the US, where she also completed a small animal internship and a residency in medical oncology. She is Professor of Clinical Pathology and Chief of Diagnostic Services at the School of Veterinary Medicine, University of Wisconsin–Madison and past Editor-in-Chief of *Veterinary Clinical Pathology*. In addition to teaching, diagnostic service, and research in clinical pathology, her interests include effective mentoring of early-career faculty and trainees, curricular development in teaching problem-solving, support of trainees in their teaching roles, and mentoring in scientific writing for publication.

Printed in the United States
By Bookmasters